Swift for the Really Impatient

Swift for the Really Impatient

Matt Henderson
Dave Wood

✦ Addison-Wesley

Upper Saddle River, NJ • Boston • Indianapolis • San Francisco
New York • Toronto • Montreal • London • Munich • Paris • Madrid
Capetown • Sydney • Tokyo • Singapore • Mexico City

Many of the designations used by manufacturers and sellers to distinguish their products are claimed as trademarks. Where those designations appear in this book, and the publisher was aware of a trademark claim, the designations have been printed with initial capital letters or in all capitals.

The authors and publisher have taken care in the preparation of this book, but make no expressed or implied warranty of any kind and assume no responsibility for errors or omissions. No liability is assumed for incidental or consequential damages in connection with or arising out of the use of the information or programs contained herein.

For information about buying this title in bulk quantities, or for special sales opportunities (which may include electronic versions; custom cover designs; and content particular to your business, training goals, marketing focus, or branding interests), please contact our corporate sales department at corpsales@pearsoned.com or (800) 382-3419.

For government sales inquiries, please contact governmentsales@pearsoned.com.

For questions about sales outside the U.S., please contact international@pearsoned.com.

Visit us on the Web: informit.com/aw

Library of Congress Control Number: 2014952492

ISBN-13: 978-0-13-396012-9
ISBN-10: 0-13-396012-9
Text printed in the United States on recycled paper at RR Donnelley in Crawfordsville, Indiana.
First printing: December 2014

Editor-in-Chief
Mark Taub

Senior Acquisitions Editor
Trina MacDonald

Development Editor
Tom Cirtin

Managing Editor
Kristy Hart

Senior Project Editor
Betsy Gratner

Copy Editor
Kitty Wilson

Indexer
Tim Wright

Proofreader
Leslie Joseph

Technical Reviewers
Rene Cacheaux
Ash Furrow

Editorial Assistant
Olivia Basegio

Cover Designer
Alan Clements

Senior Compositor
Gloria Schurick

To my mother and my father.

And to Clare.

—Matt Henderson

To my wife, Sabrina, who puts up with the crazy hours I put in and always makes sure I at least take a break for dinner.

—Dave Wood

Contents

Foreword

In March, 2008, Apple released an SDK for its wildly successful iPhone. That SDK, and the App Store that would go live several months later, attracted a lot of attention. A lot of people coming to Apple's platform for the first time were surprised to find that the entire toolset was based around an obscure 25-year-old programming language called Objective-C rather than a more widely used language like C++ or Java.

Mac developers and those who followed Apple weren't particularly surprised. Objective-C had been the primary language used to develop Mac apps since shortly after the NeXT acquisition in 1996. Unlike C++ or Java, which are general-purpose languages used on numerous platforms and for a wide variety of programming tasks, Apple chose to build first OS X and later iOS around a language that it could control. The language grew slowly and with a very singular focus on the development of GUI apps for Apple's operating systems.

In many ways, Objective-C and the NeXT frameworks used to build applications were years ahead of their time. Though never particularly successful as a commercial venture, NeXT's application-building tools were incredibly popular with those who used it because it enabled developers to build applications much faster than other tools on the market at the time.

But Objective-C is more than 30 years old now, and that's a very long time in terms of technology. While Objective-C has changed and evolved some, it really hasn't kept pace. Programming languages and compilers have evolved a lot in the last few decades, and many people have been clamoring for a more "modern" programming language for developing iOS and OS X apps.

At WWDC 2014, Apple surprised nearly everyone by announcing that it had a new modern language called Swift.

Developed in secret over the course of four years, Swift is a very different language. It has many interesting features that Objective-C lacks but uses the same run time as Objective-C and is able to use all the existing frameworks and libraries that make up the iOS and OS X SDKs.

But Swift really is different. It looks different. It feels different. You kind of even have to "think different" to use it well.

Fortunately, you've picked up just the right book to help you think different. Matt and Dave have done a great job taking you through this interesting but maybe just a little scary new language. They walk you through the how and the why and will help you steer clear of the many gotchas waiting for you as you get up to speed.

—Jeff LaMarche, author, *Beginning iPhone Development: Exploring the iPhone SDK* (Apress); managing partner and founder, MartianCraft

Preface

This book gives a concise introduction to Apple's new programming language, Swift. We've created this book for developers who are currently writing apps using Objective-C and for developers who are looking to start writing apps and are curious about what Swift offers.

This book is written in the "impatient" style and tries to mimic Cay Horstmann's style of presenting topics in a quick and clear manner that gives developers enough information to be immediately productive. The code in this book is primarily presented in short chunks designed to illustrate concepts. These code snippets are designed to act as a quick reference and do not provide a cookbook of complete examples that can be used directly.

Swift provides many exciting language features that aren't present in Objective-C, the current primary language for developing for Apple's platforms. These features are designed to make developers more productive and to make their code less prone to errors. With Swift, developers are able to make use of a strong type system and modern syntax to easily create powerful applications. Chapter 1, "Introducing Swift," and Chapter 2, "Diving Deeper into Swift's Syntax," give a rapid introduction to Swift's syntax, basic types, and features that might be new concepts for Objective-C developers. Later chapters focus more specifically on these features.

Like Objective-C, Swift is primarily an object-oriented language. Chapter 3, "Objects and Classes," introduces the major object types that are used heavily in any Swift app. Using classes in Swift will be familiar to developers who come from different object-oriented languages. In addition, Swift's type system helps prevent errors that are common with other languages.

Starting with Chapter 4, "Optionals," this book goes into slightly more depth on topics that might be less familiar to developers coming from Objective-C. Chapter 4 focuses on optional types, a new fundamental concept that forces objects to declare at the type level whether they might contain a missing or nil value. This chapter begins to explore Swift's focus on code safety. Chapter 5, "Generics," explores the concept of generics, which let developers abstract functionality for reusable code while still maintaining type safety. In Swift, functions are a first class type, which allows them to be passed around as parameters and returned as values. Chapter 6, "Functions and Closures," explores the functional programming aspects of Swift.

The main reason to learn Swift is to be able to craft apps for iOS and Mac OS X. Chapter 7, "Working with Objective-C," focuses on how to use Swift with Objective-C and Apple's existing frameworks. Swift was designed to easily integrate with existing Objective-C projects and the frameworks Apple provides for making apps, but you need to know a few important things before you try to combine Swift with C and Objective-C, and that's what Chapter 7 covers.

By the time you reach Chapter 8, "Common Patterns," you'll have a firm understanding of how to make apps using Swift and the advantages of leveraging the new features of Swift, so Chapter 8 focuses on practical use cases. Once you finish Chapter 8, you'll know how to deal with several situations that commonly come up while developing apps.

At the end of each chapter, we've included exercises that will help you develop your newly acquired skills. We encourage you to do the exercises to reinforce what you've read. If you get stuck on an exercise, please visit our website at http://SwiftForTheReallyImpatient.com, where we post solutions. You'll also find book errata and other interesting content at this site.

 NOTE

Throughout this book where a line of code is too long for the printed page, a code-continuation arrow (➡) has been used to mark the continued line of code.

Acknowledgments

Our thanks go to our editors, Trina MacDonald and Betsy Gratner, for guiding two unpublished authors through all the steps required to make this book happen. Thanks to our reviewers, Rene Cacheaux, Tom Cirtin, Ash Furrow, Kitty Wilson, and Chris Zahn, who made all the chapters read easier and made sure we kept up to date with all the Swift betas along the way. Thanks to our colleagues at MartianCraft for always offering to help, no matter how obscure the development problem, especially Jeff LaMarche for writing us a wonderful foreword and Kyle Richter for encouraging us to write this book. Finally, we'd like to thank our wives, Clare and Sabrina, for supporting us through the not entirely easy process of creating our first book.

About the Authors

Matt Henderson has been developing for Apple's platforms since 2009 and is currently a Cocoa engineer at MartianCraft. He's given several presentations at various user groups and conferences, including 360iDev, Cocoaheads Denver, and Boulder iOS Meetup. He realized he might have a future in software when he discovered it was easier for him to program his graphing calculator to solve equations than it was to study for his math tests. He thinks that the best debugging technique is taking a walk outside in the sun or snow.

Dave Wood has been developing for iOS since 2008 and OS X since 2009. He began writing code at age 9 on a TI/99/4A and instantly fell in love. He has worked on various types of projects, including systems that interface with stock exchanges, news outlets, and banking systems, as well as newspaper websites and, of course, mobile apps ranging from games, social networks, financial apps, and productivity and developer apps. When possible, he enjoys whitewater kayaking and scuba diving. Currently he runs his own development studio, Cerebral Gardens, and freelances as a Cocoa engineer for MartianCraft.

1

Introducing Swift

Topics in This Chapter

- 1.1 Basic Syntax

- 1.2 Basic Data Types

- Exercises

Swift is a new programming language developed by Apple that was released to developers at WWDC 2014. Swift can be used to develop applications for Apple's iOS and OS X platforms. It is designed to work with, but eventually replace, Objective-C, the language originally used for developing applications on Apple's platforms.

Apple has a number of goals for Swift:

- Make app development easier, with modern language features.

- Produce safer code by preventing the most common programming errors.

- Create easy-to-read code with clear and expressive syntax.

- Be compatible with existing Objective-C frameworks, including the Cocoa and Cocoa Touch frameworks.

This chapter introduces the basic syntax of Swift and lays the foundation you'll need for the rest of the book.

These are the key points in this chapter:

- You use `var` to declare a variable and `let` to declare a constant.

- You execute code conditionally with `if` or `switch` constructs.

- You repeat code segments by looping with `for`, `for-in`, `while`, and `do-while` loop constructs.

- The basic data types are implemented as `structs`, which are passed by value in code.

- Since the basic types are `structs`, they may have additional properties or methods available.

- Arrays and dictionaries in Swift are more powerful collection types than their Objective-C counterparts.

1.1 Basic Syntax

When you learn a new language, the first complete program you're likely to see is the famous "Hello World" example. In Swift, this program consists of just one line:

```
println("Hello World")
```

The first thing you should notice here is what you don't see. The code jumps right into the guts of the program. You don't need to set anything up to get started, include or import a standard library, set up an initial `main()` function to be called by the system, or even include a semicolon at the end of each line.

 NOTE

Comments in Swift are the same as in Objective-C, with one powerful addition. You can use // for a single-line comment, or you can use /* */ to surround a multiline comment. Unlike C-based languages, Swift allows you to have nested comments. This is very handy when you want to comment out a whole section of code that may already have multiline comments included. Throughout this book, we use // comments in the examples to show results and add explanations.

1.1.1 Variables and Constants

A program that only prints a static line of text isn't very useful. For a program to be useful, it needs to be able to work with data, using variables and constants. As their names imply, variables have contents that may change throughout the execution of the code, while constants cannot be changed after they're initialized. Variables are said to be *mutable*; constants are *immutable*.

In Swift, you declare a variable by using the `var` keyword, and you declare a constant by using the `let` keyword. This applies for all data types in Swift and is different from Objective-C, where the type itself indicates whether it is mutable or not, such as `NSArray` versus `NSMutableArray`. With Swift, the mutable version of an object is the same type as the immutable version—not a subclass.

For the rest of this chapter, what we say about variables applies equally to constants (provided that we're not talking about mutating data).

 NOTE

Before we look at specific types, it's important to understand that all data types in Swift are implemented as one of three different kinds of data structures. Each type is either an `enum`, a `struct`, or a `class` and thus may have properties and/or methods available. We cover these in much greater detail throughout the book, but a key fundamental you need to be aware of from the start is the difference in how these data structures are passed around in your code.

Swift employs some standard rules with regard to dealing with `enums`, `structs`, and `classes`. Whenever an `enum`, or a `struct` is passed somewhere, it is *passed by value*; that is, a copy of the original is created, and that copy is what's assigned to the new variable. This allows the new variable to be used, modified, or deleted without affecting the original. And the reverse is also true: The original can be used, modified, or deleted without affecting the new copy.

However, when a `class` is passed somewhere, it is *passed by reference*; that is, a pointer to the original variable is assigned to the new variable. Changes made to either variable will affect the other one.

All the basic types we're about to cover are implemented under the hood as `structs`, and so they are always copied and passed by value. Because they are `structs`, it's also possible for them to implement additional functionality through properties and/or methods that you wouldn't see from their Objective-C counterparts.

Swift is a strongly typed language, which means that every variable is set to a specific type at compile time, and it can only contain values of that type throughout its lifetime.

Two common types are `Int` and `Float`. (We'll get into their details a little later.) If you set a variable to be of type `Int`, it can only ever store `Int` values; it can never be coerced into storing a `Float`. Types can never be implicitly converted into other types. This means, for example, that you cannot add an `Int` to a `Float`. If you need to add two numbers together, you need to make sure they're the same type or explicitly convert one to the other. This is part of what makes Swift a safe language: The compiler prevents you from mixing types and possibly producing unexpected results.

To see the dangers involved in mixing types, consider this C code:

```
int intValue = 0;
float floatValue = 2.5;
int totalValue = intValue + floatValue;
```

This code adds an `int` and a `float` together. What would `total` be equal to here? Since the total is an `int`, it is unable to store the decimal portion of the `floatValue` variable. `floatValue` must first be implicitly converted to an `int` before it can be added to `intValue` and stored in `totalValue`. In this case, is the developer expecting the compiler to round `floatValue` to 3, or is she expecting it to just drop the decimal portion and instead add 2? Swift avoids this type of ambiguity by producing a compile-time error here, forcing you to tell it exactly what you want to happen. This is one way Swift avoids common programming errors.

You need to give variables and constants names so that you can refer to them in code. Names in Swift can be composed of most characters, including Unicode characters. While it's possible to use emoji and similar characters as variable names, you should rarely, if ever, actually do it. Here is the minimum code for declaring a variable:

```
var itemCount: Int
```

This code declares a variable named `itemCount` of type `Int`. A variable must be set to an initial value before you can use it. You can do this when the variable is declared, like this:

```
var itemCount: Int = 0
```

or you can do it at some later point, as long as you do it before you attempt to read the value.

Swift has a feature called *type inference*. If the compiler has enough information from the initial value you set to infer the type, you can omit the type of the variable when you declare it. For example, if your variable is going to be an `Int`, you can declare it like this:

```
var itemCount = 0
```

Because 0 is an `Int`, `itemCount` is inferred to be an `Int`. This is exactly the same as the example above. The compiler generates exactly the same machine code.

If the variable's initial value is set to the return value of a function, the compiler will infer the type to be the same as the return value's type.

Given a function `numberOfItems()` that returns an `Int` and the following line:

```
var itemCount = numberOfItems()
```

the compiler will infer `itemCount` to be of type `Int`.

Since the compiler generates exactly the same code whether you explicitly set the type or use type inference to let the compiler set the type for you, there is no advantage or disadvantage to either method at run time. Of course, if you need to explicitly set the type, you have no option. But in cases where the compiler can infer the type, it's up to you whether to let the compiler do so or whether you explicitly set the type anyway. There are two things to consider when making this decision. The first is readability. If, when you use type inference, the type of the variable would still be clear to a future reader of the code, by all means save some keystrokes and use type inference. If the initial value being set is the return value of some uncommon function, it may be clearer to the future reader if you explicitly set the type. When reading the code at a later date, you don't want to have to look up what a function returns just to determine a variable's type.

The second reason you might want to explicitly set a type when it can be inferred is to add an additional safety check. This ensures that the type you're expecting the variable to be and the type being set match. If there's a mismatch, you get a compile-time error and can make the necessary corrections.

1.1.2 String Interpolation

You've already seen how to print a line of text to the console by using the `println` command. You can add variables, constants, and other expressions to the output by using string interpolation. You do so by including variables and expressions directly in the string literal, surrounded by parentheses and escaped with a backslash:

```
var fileCount = 99
println("There are \(fileCount) files in your folder")
//outputs: There are 99 files in your folder
```

This doesn't apply just to `println`. You can use it anywhere a string literal is used:

```
var firstName = "Geoff"
var lastName = "Cawthorne"
var username = "\(firstName)\(lastName)\(arc4random() % 500)"
//username: GeoffCawthorne253
```

1.1.3 Control Flow

All but the simplest of programs require some sort of logic to determine what actions should be taken. Decisions must be made based on the information the program has available. Logic such as "If this, do that" or "Do this *x* many times" determines the flow of an app and, thus, its result.

Conditionals

Swift offers both `if` and `switch` constructs for you to execute code conditionally.

Using `if` is the simpler of the two constructs and closely follows what you're used to in Objective-C. There are a few differences you need to be aware of, however. The first difference continues Swift's theme of reducing unnecessary syntax: Swift does not require you to surround test expressions with parentheses, though you may, if you desire. The second difference is that braces are required around the conditional code. Third, the test expression must explicitly result in a `true` or `false` answer; an `Int` variable with a value of `0` is not implicitly evaluated as `false`, nor is a value of anything else implicitly evaluated as `true`.

Here is a minimal example:

```
var daysUntilEvent: Int = calculateDaysUntilEvent()
if daysUntilEvent > 0 {
    println("There is still time to buy a gift")
}
```

You can chain together multiple `if`s with the `else` keyword:

```
var daysUntilEvent: Int = calculateDaysUntilEvent()
if daysUntilEvent > 0 {
    println("There is still time to buy a gift")
}
else if daysUntilEvent < 0 {
    println("You missed it, better pick up a belated card")
}
else {
    println("Better pick up the gift on the way")
}
```

The `switch` construct is an alternative to `if` statements. It is based on what you've used in Objective-C, but in Swift, it is much more powerful. There are two important differences you need to consider when using a `switch` in Swift. The first is that every possible option must be covered. A `default` case can be used to accomplish this requirement. The second difference is a major change in how cases are handled. In C-based languages, you need to include a `break` statement at the end of each case, or execution will continue with the next case. This has been the source of many errors over time. To prevent these errors in Swift, the design was changed to automatically break when the next case begins. Some algorithms may require the old behavior, so it is available to you through the use of the `fallthrough` keyword.

Here's a basic example of a `switch` in use:

```
var numberOfItemsInCart: Int = calculateNumberOfItemsInCart()
switch numberOfItemsInCart {
case 0:
    println("Cart is Empty")
case 1:
    println("1 item in cart, standard shipping applies")
default:
    println("\(numberOfItemsInCart) items, you quality for free
➥shipping")
}
```

We'll cover advanced `switch` usage in Chapter 2, "Diving Deeper into Swift's Syntax."

Loops

In Swift, `for`, `for-in`, `while`, and `do-while` are used for looping. These are similar to what you're used to in Objective-C, with only slight differences in the syntax.

Here is a basic `for` example:

```
for var i = 0; i < 10; ++i {
    println("i = \(i)")
}
```

Just as with `if` statements, you can omit the parentheses. In this example, `i` is implicitly declared as an `Int`. The loop will iterate while `i < 10`, and it's incremented by 1 at the end of each iteration.

Another form of the `for` loop is the `for-in` loop. This lets you iterate through each item in a collection, such as an array or a range.

Swift has two new range operators for creating ranges that can be used with for-in loops. The ..< operator is the half-open range operator; it includes the value on the left side but not the value on the right side. Here's an example that iterates 10 times, with i starting as 0 and ending as 9:

```
for i in 0 ..< 10 {
    println("i = \(i)")
}
```

The ... operator is the inclusive range operator. It includes the values on both sides. This example iterates 10 times, with i starting as 1 and ending as 10:

```
for i in 1 ... 10 {
    println("i = \(i)")
}
```

When you use a for-in loop to iterate through a collection such as an Array, it looks like this:

```
var itemIds: [Int] = generateItemIds()
for itemId in itemIds {
    println("itemId: \(itemId)")
}
```

The while loop iterates for as long as the test condition is true. If the test condition is false at the start, the loop doesn't iterate at all, and it is just skipped entirely. For instance, this example will never actually print 100% complete since the test condition becomes false once percentComplete == 100:

```
var percentComplete: Float = calculatePercentComplete()
while percentComplete < 100 {
    println("\(percentComplete)% complete")
    percentComplete = calculatePercentComplete()
}
```

If you change this to a do-while loop, the test condition is evaluated at the end of the loop. This guarantees that the loop will iterate at least once and also means it will iterate a final time when the test condition fails (which could be the first iteration). This version updates the display one final time once the task being monitored is complete:

```
var percentComplete: Float = 0.0
do {
    percentComplete = calculatePercentComplete()
    println("\(percentComplete)% complete")
} while percentComplete < 100
```

When using a loop, there are times when you need to adjust the iterations by either quitting iteration altogether or skipping a single iteration. Just as in Objective-C, there are two keywords you can use for these purposes: break and continue. You use break to immediately jump out of the loop and cancel any further iterations:

```
var percentComplete: Float = 0.0
do {
    percentComplete = calculatePercentComplete()
    if taskCancelled() {
        println("cancelled")
        break
    }
    println("\(percentComplete)% complete")
} while percentComplete < 100
```

You use continue to end the current iteration and immediately start the next one:

```
var filesToDownload: [SomeFileClass] = filesNeeded()
for file in filesToDownload {
    if file.alreadyDownloaded {
        continue
    }

    file.download()
}
```

With nested loops, break and continue affect only the inner loop. Swift has a powerful feature that Objective-C does not have: You can add labels to your loops and then specify which loop you would like to break or continue out of. A label consists of the name followed by a colon in front of the loop keyword:

```
var folders: [SomeFolderClass] = foldersToProcess()
outer: for folder in folders {
    inner: for file in folder.files {
        if shouldCancel() {
```

```
        break outer
    }

    file.process()
    }
}
```

1.2 Basic Data Types

Swift has a standard set of basic data types for storing numbers, strings, and Boolean values.

By convention, types in Swift are named using camel case notation. Unlike in Objective-C, there is no prefix (NS, CG, etc.) on the standard type names.

1.2.1 `Int`

For storing integer values, the basic type is `Int`. It is 32 bits deep on 32-bit devices and 64 bits deep on 64-bit devices.

You can access the minimum and maximum values the type can store by using the `min` and `max` static properties:

```
println("\(Int.min)")
//output on 32-bit device: -2147483648
//output on 64-bit device: -9223372036854775808

println("\(Int.max)")
//output on 32-bit device: 2147483647
//output on 64-bit device: 9223372036854775807
```

When you need an integer with a specific bit depth, you use `Int8`, `Int16`, `Int32`, or `Int64`.

There are also unsigned variants of the `Int` types. You can prefix the `Int` type name with a `U` to get the corresponding unsigned version: `UInt8`, `UInt16`, `UInt32`, or `UInt64`.

Because Swift is a strongly typed language, you can't mix and match these `Int` types haphazardly. You cannot even do basic math or comparisons with mixed types. In Objective-C it's common to see `NSUInteger` values assigned to or compared with an `NSInteger`, with little regard for a possible overflow. This is especially common when using the `count` property on an `NSArray` variable:

```
for (NSInteger i = 0; i < [someNSArray count]; ++i) {
    NSLog(@"%@", someNSArray[i]);
}
```

Since `NSArray`'s `count` method actually returns an `NSUInteger` value, this example compares two different types. It even passes in the wrong type to the array's subscript. This is a bug just waiting to go BOOM!—most likely after you've shipped the app, and a user has more data than you imagined or tested with, thus hitting an overflow.

This sort of bug just can't happen with Swift. The compiler won't let you mix unsigned and signed values, and it won't let you mix variables with different bit depths. Nor will it let you assign one type to another. For this reason, Apple recommends that you always use the `Int` type unless you specifically need a certain bit depth or have to use an unsigned value (perhaps for really large numbers). This helps you avoid having to convert one `Int` type to another. Apple has modified the Cocoa classes to follow this guideline. As mentioned earlier in this chapter, in Objective-C, `NSArray`'s `count` property returns an `NSUInteger` (unsigned), but in Swift it returns an `Int` (signed), even though it can never be negative.

In cases in which you need to convert from one type to another, you can do so by creating a new instance of the destination type, using the original value as its initial value:

```
var a32BitInt: Int32 = 10
var a64BitInt: Int64 = Int64(a32BitInt)
//a64BitInt: 10 (in a 64-bit variable)
```

This works by creating a new `Int64` with an initial value of `a32BitInt`.

Be careful, however, because this can create overflow situations. The compiler will catch obvious overflows for you, but it cannot catch all instances, like this:

```
var a64BitInt: Int64 = Int64.max
var a32BitInt: Int32 = Int32(a64BitInt)
//error: a32BitInt overflows
```

CAUTION

To ensure compatibility when transferring files between devices, any integer variables that you're writing to a file (or transmitting across a network) should explicitly specify the bit depth. You should force the use of either 32- or 64-bit variables to avoid possible type mismatches and/or corruption of the data when reading in the saved values. If you store an `Int` on a 32-bit device and then read it in on a 64-bit device, bad things can happen. Even if your app doesn't allow for transferring of files, a user can still restore settings originally stored on a 32-bit device to a new 64-bit device and then encounter the same problem. Use `Int32`, `UInt32`, `Int64`, or `UInt64` for values you need to save.

1.2.2 `Double` **and** `Float`

When you need to work with decimal numbers in Swift, you can work with `Float` and `Double`. `Float` is always a 32-bit value, while `Double` is always a 64-bit value, regardless of the device architecture.

When using decimal literal values, the compiler always infers a `Double` type and not a `Float`. Therefore, if you don't need the precision of a 64-bit value, you should explicitly declare the variable as a `Float`, like this:

```
var distance = 0.0
//distance is a Double
var seconds: Float = 0.0
//seconds is a Float
```

The following examples show some useful properties. These examples use a `Float`, but they would work just the same with a `Double`:

```
var someFloat = Float.NaN
if someFloat.isNaN {
    println("someFloat is not a number")
}


someFloat = Float.infinity
if someFloat.isInfinite {
    println("someFloat is equal to infinity")
}
```

```
someFloat = -Float.infinity
if someFloat.isInfinite {
    println("someFloat is equal to infinity,")
    println("even though it's really negative infinity")
}
if someFloat.isInfinite && someFloat.isSignMinus {
    println("someFloat is equal to negative infinity")
}


someFloat = 0/0
if someFloat.isNaN {
    println("someFloat is not a number")
    println("note, we divided by zero and did not crash!")
}
```

1.2.3 Bool

The `Bool` type stores Boolean values and is very similar to what you're used to in Objective-C. However, Swift uses `true` and `false` rather than Objective-C's YES and NO.

In Objective-C, pretty much anything can be converted to a Boolean. If it is something, it's treated as YES, and if it is nothing (e.g., `nil`), it's NO. Here's an example:

```
NSInteger someInteger = 0;
BOOL hasSome = someInteger;
//hasSome: NO
someInteger = 100;
hasSome = someInteger;
//hasSome: YES
NSObject* someObject = nil;
BOOL isValidObject = someObject;
//isValidObject: NO
```

This is not the case with Swift. With Swift, only expressions that explicitly return a `Bool` may be used to define a `Bool` value. You can't implicitly compare values to 0 or `nil`. Here's an example:

```
var someInteger = 0
var hasSome:Bool = (someInteger != 0)
//hasSome: false
```

```
someInteger = 100
hasSome = (someInteger != 0)
//hasSome = true
```

1.2.4 Strings

Strings in Swift are very different from strings in Objective-C. In Swift, `String` literals are simply text surrounded by double quotes:

```
var greetingString = "Hello World"
```

A `String` is implemented as a collection of `Characters`. Each `Character` represents a Unicode character, one of more than 110,000 characters and symbols from more than 100 scripts. `Characters` are implemented with one of several character encoding methods, such as UTF-8 or UTF-16. These encoding methods use a variable number of bytes in memory to store each character. Because characters vary in size, you cannot determine the length of a string by looking at its size in memory, as you can in Objective-C. Instead, you must use the `countElements()` function to determine how many characters are in a `String`. `countElements` iterates through the string and looks at each character to determine the count. While Swift's `String` is compatible with Objective-C's `NSString`, and you can use `String` wherever `NSString` is called for, the implementations are different, and thus the element count may not be the same value you would get from the `NSString` `length` property. This is because `length` returns the number of 16-bit code units in the UTF-16 version of the `NSString`, and some Unicode characters use more than 1. You can use the `utf16Count` property of a `String` to access the `NSStrings` `length` equivalent:

```
var myPuppy = "Harlow looks just like this: 🐶"
println("\(countElements(myPuppy))")
//output: 30
println("\(myPuppy.utf16Count)")
//output: 31, 🐶 uses 2 16-bit code units
```

You can concatenate `Strings` together by using the + operator:

```
var firstName = "Sabrina"
var lastName = "Wood"
var displayName = firstName + " " + lastName
//displayName: Sabrina Wood
```

You can also append one string to another by using the `+=` operator:

```
var name = "Katelyn"
name += " Millington"
//name: Katelyn Millington
```

Since a `String` is a collection of `Characters`, you can iterate through them by using a `for-in` loop:

```
var originalMessage = "Secret Message"
var unbreakableCode = ""
for character in originalMessage {
    unbreakableCode = String(character) + unbreakableCode
}
//unbreakableCode: egasseM terceS
```

Notice that you cannot concatenate a `Character` and a `String` together. You must create a new `String` that contains the character and concatenate that to the `unbreakableCode` variable.

The syntax for comparing strings is also much improved in Swift over Objective-C. For example, compare the following Objective-C code:

```
NSString* enteredPasswordHash = @"someSaltedHash";
NSString* storedPasswordHash = @"someSaltedHash";
BOOL accessGranted = [enteredPasswordHash isEqualToString:
➥storedPasswordHash];
//accessGranted: YES
```

to this Swift code:

```
var enteredPasswordHash = "someSaltedHash"
var storedPasswordHash = "someSaltedHash"
var accessGranted = (enteredPasswordHash == storedPasswordHash)
//accessGranted: true
```

1.2.5 Arrays

Arrays are one of the collection types offered in Swift. An array is an ordered list of items of the same type. In Swift, when you declare an array, you must specify what type it will contain. Once you've done that, it can contain only that type. This ensures that when you pull an item out of the array, you're guaranteed to have the type you expect.

To create an array literal, you surround a list of elements with square brackets, like this:

```
var dogs = ["Harlow", "Cliff", "Rusty", "Mia", "Bailey"]
```

Be sure that all elements are of the same type, or you will receive a compile-time error.

There are two ways to indicate the type of an array: the long form and the short form. These two ways are equivalent and can be used interchangeably:

- Long form: `Array<ValueType>`

- Short form: `[ValueType]`

The syntax to declare and initialize an array using the short form is:

```
var people: [String] = [] //explicit type
//or, alternately
var people = [String]() //implicit type
```

This example declares an array variable called `people`, which will contain `String` values, and you initialize it to an empty array.

You can use type inference to let the compiler determine the types of objects in the array, provided that you give enough information when you declare it:

```
let bosses = ["Jeff", "Kyle", "Marcus", "Rob", "Sabrina"]
```

Because you're initializing the array with strings, the compiler infers that `bosses` is an array of type `[String]`.

 NOTE

When you create an immutable array in Swift, you cannot add, change, or remove any items in that array. You can, however, change properties on the elements of the array.

Given an array variable, there are several key methods you can use to access or modify the contents:

```
var primaryIds: [Int] = [1, 2, 3]
//primaryIds: [1, 2, 3]
println(primaryIds.count)
//output: 3
primaryIds.append(4)
//primaryIds: [1, 2, 3, 4]
```

```
primaryIds.insert(5, atIndex:0)
//primaryIds: [5, 1, 2, 3, 4]
primaryIds.removeAtIndex(1)
//primaryIds: [5, 2, 3, 4]
primaryIds.removeLast()
//primaryIds: [5, 2, 3]
primaryIds.removeAll()
//primaryIds: []
println(primaryIds.isEmpty)
//output: true
```

You can also use subscripting to access a specific element or range of elements:

```
var primaryIds: [Int] = [1, 2, 3]
//primaryIds: [1, 2, 3]
println(primaryIds[2])
//output: 3 (arrays are zero based)
primaryIds[2] = 12
//primaryIds: [1, 2, 12]
primaryIds[0...1] = [10]
//primaryIds: [10, 12]
//notice the [] surrounding the 10
println(primaryIds[3])
//error: 3 is beyond the bounds (0...2) of the array
```

Make sure you don't attempt to access an element that is beyond the bounds of the array, though, or you'll encounter a run-time error, and your app will crash.

There are some important differences between the Objective-C NSArrays that you're used to and arrays in Swift. In Objective-C, you can only store objects that are of type NSObject (or a subclass) in an NSArray. This is why classes such as NSNumber exist: They're object wrappers around basic types so you can use them in collections. You don't add 3 to an NSArray; you add an NSNumber with a value set to 3 to the array. In Swift, you can add structs, enums, or classes to an array, and because all the base types are implemented as structs, they can all be easily added directly to an array, including literals such as 3. What happens when they are added to the array, however, differs depending on the type that is added. Recall the rules we discussed earlier, about how Swift passes structs compared to how it passes classes. These rules come into play when you're adding objects to an array. If you add an enum or a struct to an array, you add a copy, not a reference to the original object. If you add a class, however, you add a reference to the object. The same rules apply when you pass an array. The array itself is copied because it is a `struct`, and then each element is either copied or referenced, depending on whether it is an `enum`, a `struct`, or a `class`.

This means you can alter what elements are in each array independently, without affecting another array. If the elements are `enums` or `structs`, you can also alter them independently. If the elements are `classes`, changing one element will have an effect on the same element in the other array (as well as that object if it exists outside the array).

Here you can see these concepts in action:

```
var coordA = CGPoint(x: 1, y: 1)
var coordB = CGPoint(x: 2, y: 2)
var coords = [coordA, coordB]
//coordA/B are copied into the coords array
//coords: [{x 1 y 1}, {x 2 y 2}]
var copyOfCoords = coords
//copyOfCoords: [{x 1 y 1}, {x 2 y 2}]
coordA.x = 4
//coordA: {x 4 y 1}
//coords and copyOfCoords are unchanged
//coords: [{x 1 y 1}, {x 2 y 2}]
coords[0].x = 10
//coords: [{x 10 y 1}, {x 2 y 2}]
//copyOfCoords is unchanged, because each element is a struct
//copyOfCoords: [{x 1 y 1}, {x 2 y 2}]
```

Because arrays are collections, you can iterate over the contents by using a `for-in` loop:

```
for coord in coords {
    println("Coord(\(coord.x), \(coord.y))")
}
```

You can also use the `enumerate()` function to access an array index inside the for-in loop:

```
for (index, coord) in enumerate(coords) {
    println("Coord[\(index)](\(coord.x), \(coord.y))")
}
```

1.2.6 Dictionaries

A *dictionary* is an unordered collection of items of a specific type, each associated with a unique key.

As with arrays, there are two ways to indicate the type of a dictionary: the long form and the short form. These two ways are equivalent and can be used interchangeably:

- Long form: `Dictionary<KeyType, ValueType>`

- Short form: `[KeyType: ValueType]`

The syntax to declare and initialize a dictionary using the short form is:

```
var people: [String:SomePersonClass] = [:] //explicit type
//or, alternately
var people = [String:SomePersonClass]() //implicit type
```

This example declares a dictionary variable called `people`, which will contain `SomePersonClass` values associated with `String` keys, and you initialize it to an empty dictionary.

You can use type inference to let the compiler determine the types of objects in the dictionary when assigning a dictionary literal during the declaration:

```
var highScores = ["Dave":101, "Aaron":102]
```

Because you're initializing the dictionary with keys and values, the compiler infers that the `highScores` variable is a dictionary of type `[String:Int]`.

You can use any type that conforms to the `Hashable` protocol as the `KeyType` value. All of Swift's basic types are hashable by default, so any of them can be used as a key.

You can access and/or manipulate specific values in a dictionary with subscripting:

```
println(highScores["Dave"])
//output: Optional(101)
highScores["Sarah"] = 103
//added a new player
println(highScores["Sarah"])
//output: Optional(103)
//Don't worry about the Optional() portion of the output.
//We introduce that in Chapter 2, "Diving Deeper into
//Swift's Syntax."
```

Because a dictionary is a collection, you can iterate through it with a `for-in` loop:

```
for (playerName, playerScore) in highScores {
    println("\(playerName): \(playerScore)")
}
```

You can determine the number of elements in a dictionary by using the `count` property. Dictionaries also have two array properties, `keys` and `values`, that can be iterated through independently.

Exercises

1. Declare and initialize a pair of variables for each type listed in this chapter, both explicitly and using type inference. What do you need to do to get the compiler to infer the `Float` type?

2. Create a constant with an emoji character in the name. Are you able to easily use the constant? Does this help with the readability of your code?

3. How would you explicitly declare an array that stores another array of `Ints` as each element? Show how you would access elements by using subscripts.

4. Set up a dictionary that uses `Ints` as the key. How is this different from using an array? When could using a dictionary such as this be better than using an array?

5. Create a Fizz Buzz implementation. Iterate through the numbers from 1 to 100. If a number is evenly divisible by 3, print Fizz. If the number is evenly divisible by 5, print Buzz. If the number is evenly divisible by both 3 and 5, print Fizz Buzz. For all other numbers, just print the number.

Diving Deeper into Swift's Syntax

Topics in This Chapter

- 2.1 Optionals

- 2.2 Generics

- 2.3 Type Annotations and Type Inference

- 2.4 Functions and Closures

- 2.5 Tuples

- 2.6 `switch` Statements and Pattern Matching

- Exercises

To help programmers be more efficient, Swift has concise and expressive syntax. It is also designed to produce safer code by providing ways to avoid common bugs. In this chapter you will learn some of the ways you can take advantage of Swift's syntax to clearly create programs and take advantage of the safe patterns that Swift introduces to make your code more stable and less prone to errors.

These are the key points in this chapter:

- Optionals allow you to safely work with values that might not be present.

- Generics help you write expressive, reusable code that maintains type safety.

- Swift's type annotation and type inference help you write more concise code without sacrificing type safety.

- Closures provide a powerful way of isolating code, and you can easily use functions in Swift as both parameters and return values.

- Tuples provide a simple and flexible way to work with multiple related pieces of data.

- Switch statements, in conjunction with pattern matching, enable expressive and safe control flow.

2.1 Optionals

Many times, the value of a variable may or may not exist, and incorrectly handling missing values can result in errors in code. Trying to read a value from a database that has been deleted and trying to get data from a network service and encountering an authentication error are two reasons out of a limitless number of possible situations in which expected data is missing. You need to handle such situations correctly in order to create stable apps. To handle these types of cases, Swift provides optionals. An optional provides a safe way to check whether a value is present, and if so, to access that value.

An optional can represent two different cases at runtime: `Some` or `None`. With optionals, either you have a value, which is represented as `Optional.Some(value)`, or you do not have a valid value, which is represented as `Optional.None`. When your variable needs to represent both cases, you must specify that a variable is an optional by adding `?` to its type signature (so, for example, `Int` would become `Int?`). You can use optionals for all types, not just classes.

A common data structure that uses optionals is `Dictionary`. `Dictionary` returns an optional when you use subscripts to access values because the value for a key might not exist:

```
let dict = ["Henderson":"Matt"]
let firstName = dict["Henderson"]
//firstName is inferred to be an Optional String: String?
```

An optional provides a wrapper around a value and cannot be used the same way as a non-optional value. For example, you can't use `String?` in places that expect `String`:

```
let greeting = "Hello " + firstName
//error: value of optional type 'String?' not unwrapped
```

If you need to access the value, you have to *un*wrap the value by using `!` on the variable:

```
let greeting = "Hello " + firstName!
//greeting: String = "Hello Matt"
```

However, if you try to unwrap a value that doesn't exist at runtime, like this, your app will crash:

```
let daveFirstName = dict["Wood"]

//daveFirstName is nil

let daveFirstNameString = daveFirstName!

//error: Can't unwrap Optional.None
```

Optionals force you to be conscious of where values might be missing by not allowing normal data types to be assigned nonexistent values. This is very different from the normal patterns in Objective-C of returning nil or a sentinel value like NSNotFound to represent missing data. Objective-C has no built-in safeguards against a method returning nil and then trying to use nil where it isn't allowed. Swift eliminates these situations by not allowing non-optionals to be nil. Trying to set a type that isn't optional to nil results in a compile-time error:

```
var nonOptionalVariable = "ok"

nonOptionalVariable = nil

//error: this code will not compile
```

With Objective-C, you can set any object pointer to nil, and you've probably run into an error when you've expected a valid object and encountered nil. For example, say you have a method like this that returns nil in certain situations:

```
- (NSNumber*)nextNumber:(NSInteger)someNumber {

    if (someNumber >= 0) {

        return @(someNumber+1);

    }


    return nil;

}
```

Now add the return value from that method to a mutable array:

```
NSMutableArray* numbers = [NSMutableArray array];

[numbers addObject:[self nextNumber:1]];

[numbers addObject:[self nextNumber:-1]];

//error: Executing this line will result in a crash
```

This is an example of the situations that are mostly eliminated with optionals in Swift. Here's what the previous code would look like using optionals:

```
func nextNumber(num: Int) -> Int? {
    if num >= 0 {
        return num + 1
    }


    return nil
}
var numbers = [Int]()
numbers.append(nextNumber(1))
//error: value of optional type 'Int?' not unwrapped
```

> **NOTE**
>
> You could also write this example by specifying the optional cases of `Some` and `None` directly:
>
> ```
> func nextNumber(num: Int) -> Int? {
>     if num >= 0 {
>         return .Some(num + 1)
>     }
>
>     return .None
> }
> ```

The compiler will catch this situation and force the optional value that is returned by `nextNumber` to be checked for validity before being added to the array. To get the code to compile, you need to unwrap the optional, and because you don't want to ignore the potential of it being a `None` value, you check the returned value before unwrapping it:

```
var nextInt = nextNumber(-1)
if nextInt != nil {
    var validNextInt = nextInt!
    numbers.append(validNextInt)
}
```

Having to check that an optional contains a value and then unwrapping the optional would very quickly create code that is overly verbose. Swift strives to produce compact and readable code, and it offers an elegant way to check and unwrap optionals in one step. This concept is called *optional binding*, and it creates a short but safe way to work with data. For example, this code:

```
if someOptional != nil {
    let someValue = someOptional!
    //use someValue
}
```

can be written in this single statement that uses optional binding:

```
if let someValue = someOptional {
    //use someValue
}
```

Using optionals is discussed in greater detail in Chapter 4, "Optionals."

2.2 Generics

Swift provides many powerful features that exist in other programming languages but are missing from Objective-C. One such feature is generics. You can use generics to create expressive, reusable code that maintains type safety. By using generics, you can reduce code duplication and also leverage Swift's powerful type system to create expressive, abstract functions and objects. This section takes a look at how generics can be used.

Say that you have a method that takes two Int objects and returns the greater of the two:

```
func maxInt(lhs: Int, rhs: Int) -> Int {
    if lhs > rhs {
        return lhs
    }
    return rhs
}
```

You can only call this function with Int parameters, so if you want to have the same functionality for Double values, you would need to create a new function, like this:

```
func maxDouble(lhs: Double, rhs: Double) -> Double {
    if lhs > rhs {
        return lhs
    }


    return rhs
}
```

This will work, but look at the two function bodies. You can see that you are duplicating a lot of code. If this were a more complicated function and the implementation ever changed, you'd have to make sure that all changes were made to each version. If you wanted to handle floats later on, you would need to duplicate the function again, and this problem of duplication would snowball for every type that a function needed to support. Generics offer a simple solution:

```
func maxValue<T: Comparable>(lhs: T, rhs: T) -> T {
    if lhs > rhs {
        return lhs
    }


    return rhs
}
```

The only part of the function you had to change is the signature:

```
func maxValue<T: Comparable>(lhs: T, rhs: T) -> T
```

In this line, you are declaring a new function and giving the function the name maxValue, as if it's any normal function, but before the parameter list, you've added <T:Comparable>, which is where you declare that this is a generic function. <T:Comparable> tells the compiler that the function will have a generic type T that implements Comparable (the protocol that defines the function > used in the body). In this function definition, T acts as a placeholder type to be filled in with the specific type when the function is actually called. After creating a generic function, you can call it with any values that match the requirements of the generic type. Every specific type that needs to use this function will result in a different function, but this is handled by the compiler.

Programming with generics allows you to abstract the behavior of your functions and focus on what's important while letting the compiler make sure your code works correctly with respect to types. Swift's standard library uses generics to provide many useful functions and classes. `Array` and `Dictionary` are both just generic collections. Here's the structure definition of `Array`:

```
struct Array<T>: MutableCollection, Sliceable
```

When you look at the type of an array after it is created, you can see that it is specific to a type:

```
let numbers = [1, 2, 3]
//numbers: [Int]
let strings = ["a", "b", "c"]
//strings: [String]
```

Typed collections provide a built-in level of safety by not allowing the addition of elements that don't fulfill the type requirements. Also, elements pulled from the collection will be of a known type (wrapped in an optional). Knowing that all elements of a collection conform to a specific type also means that you can be confident of the behavior when processing elements in the collection. Here's an example of a simple function that computes the sum of an array of `Ints`:

```
func sum(nums: [Int]) -> Int {
    var sum = 0
    for num in nums {
        sum += num
    }
    return sum
}
```

There is no need to examine each individual element to make sure it is an `Int` because you know that the compiler has already done that check for you. If you accidentally try to add a value that doesn't belong, you will be notified immediately by a compiler error instead of running into a crash when the incorrect type is treated like an `Int`:

```
var randomNumbers = [2, 5, 14, 17, 22, 81, 96]
let notANumber = "1"
randomNumbers.append(notANumber)
//error: 'NSString' is not a subtype of 'Int'
```

Generics are a very powerful feature of Swift that we look at in more detail in Chapter 5, "Generics."

2.3 Type Annotations and Type Inference

Two of the guiding principles behind the design of Swift are making the developer more productive and making the code that's produced safer to execute. Swift's typing system and the type inference provided by the compiler allow you to create safe code with a fraction of the amount of typing that would be required in other statically typed languages. Here's an example of what Swift looks like without using type inference:

```
var stringIntDictionay: Dictionary<String, Int> =
➥Dictionary<String, Int>()
stringIntDictionay.updateValue(1, forKey: "one")
```

This short example creates a dictionary that requires keys to be of type `String` and values to be of type `Int`. Notice how it uses the generics syntax to specify which types this dictionary can be used with. If you try to add a `Double` to this dictionary, you get an error. This is great for creating safer code, but it's messy to read and requires a lot of typing, which is unnecessary and unproductive. The Swift compiler enables you to write very concise code without requiring you to specify type information when all the type information is obvious. The following code achieves the same result as above but is much easier to understand:

```
var stringIntDictionay = ["one":1]
//stringIntDictionay: Dictionary<String, Int>
```

The compiler can use the initial set of data, `["one":1]`, to infer the necessary type information needed to define the dictionary.

Sometimes it isn't possible for the compiler to infer the right information. In such situations, you can specify the type directly. The following example shows how to create a custom protocol and some variables of objects that implement the protocol:

```
protocol Speaks {
    func speak() -> String
}


struct Duck: Speaks {
    func speak() -> String {
        return "quack"
    }
}
```

```
struct Dog: Speaks {
    func speak() -> String {
        return "bark"
    }
}


let fido = Dog()
let donald = Duck()
```

If you try to create an array with the constants `fido` and `donald` without declaring a type for the array, you encounter an error.

```
let pets = [fido, donald]
//error: cannot convert the expression's type 'Array' to type
//'ArrayLiteralConvertible'
```

This produces an error because the compiler cannot infer a type for this array, and all arrays must be typed. Here is how you can fix the problem:

```
let pets:[Speaks] = [fido, donald]
```

You declare the type of the array directly, and then the compiler only needs to make sure that `fido` and `donald` both conform to the type requirements, which in this example means implementing the `Speaks` protocol. Thanks to Swift's requirements for type information combined with the smart type inferencing of the compiler, you can write code that doesn't sacrifice safety for readability; you get both.

2.4 Functions and Closures

The capability to isolate pieces of code is important for creating clean, useful code. Swift gives you this capability through the use of closures. Closures provide a way of creating self-contained pieces of functionality that can also capture values from their defining context. The term closure comes from this capability to capture variables and constants from the existing context, which is known as closing over the values. Swift's closures are similar to Objective-C's blocks but provide more flexibility in their uses. In addition, the syntax for closures is much simpler in many cases. Closures come in three different flavors that each fulfills a slightly different purpose: global functions, nested functions, and closure expressions.

2.4.1 Global Functions

Global functions are the most common type of closure; a global function includes a name and doesn't capture any values. You create a global function by using the `func` keyword followed by the name of the function, a comma-separated list of parameters inside parentheses, and optionally `->` followed by a return type. For example, here's a basic function that doesn't take any parameters or return a value:

```
func globalFunction() {
    println("hello")
}
```

 NOTE

Functions that do not declare a return type return `Void`, which represents an empty tuple: `()`.

2.4.2 Nested Functions

Functions can also be nested inside other functions. Nested functions cannot be called directly from outside their declaring context but can have their functionality exposed by being returned from a function. Unlike a global function, which does not capture any values, a nested function can capture values from its enclosing function. Here's an example of a nested function:

```
func greetingMaker(greeting: String) -> (String -> String) {
    func greetFunc(name: String) -> String {
        return "\(greeting), \(name)"
    }
    return greetFunc
}

var hiGreeting = greetingMaker("Hi")
println(hiGreeting("Dave"))
//Hi, Dave
var heyGreeting = greetingMaker("Hey")
println(heyGreeting("Matt"))
//Hey, Matt
```

Nested functions automatically have access to all variables and constants defined in their enclosing function. Here's a simple nested function that uses a variable defined in the outer function:

```
func makeCounter(increment: Int) -> (() -> Int) {
    //each time makeCounter is called a new
    //count variable is created and captured
    var count = 0
    func counter() -> Int {
        count += increment
        return count
    }
    return counter
}

var oneCount = makeCounter(1)
var tenCount = makeCounter(10)
println(oneCount())
//1
println(tenCount())
//10
println(oneCount())
//2
println(tenCount())
//20
```

2.4.3 Closure Expressions

Closure expressions provide a lightweight way of isolating code by not requiring the block of code to be named and also enable values to be captured from the context. Here's an example of a simple closure expression:

```
var aFewNumbers = [1, 2, 3]
var squares = aFewNumbers.map({ (num: Int) -> Int in
    return num * num } )
//[1, 4, 9]
```

You can see from this example that the syntax is very similar to that of global and nested functions. Inside a set of braces you define a list of parameters, a return type, and the keyword in, followed by the statements of the closure:

```
{ (parameters) -> return type in
    statements
}
```

Swift also provides many ways to write closures in a cleaner and more concise manner. Read more about it in Chapter 6, "Functions and Closures."

2.5 Tuples

A tuple is a small and powerful data structure in Swift that allows you to combine multiple values into a single entity. Tuples are flexible in what they can store, allowing each value to be of a different type, as well as variable length. Tuples provide a natural way of structuring related pieces of data without the overhead of creating classes. You create a tuple by supplying a comma-separated list of values inside parentheses. Here's a simple example:

```
let iceCreamCone = (2, "chocolate", "cone")
//iceCreamCone: (Int, String, String)
```

To pull the data out of a tuple, you can access the values by index or you can decompose the values in the tuple into individual variables. Here's what these techniques look like:

```
println("I'd like \(iceCreamCone.0) scoop(s) of
➡\(iceCreamCone.1) in a \(iceCreamCone.2)")
//I'd like 2 scoop(s) of chocolate in a cone


let (scoops, flavor, style) = iceCreamCone
println("I'd like \(scoops) scoop(s) of \(flavor)
➡in a \(style)")
//I'd like 2 scoop(s) of chocolate in a cone
```

You can also create tuples with named values, and those names can then be used to extract the values. This provides a simple way of adding clarity to a tuple's data and is a lightweight alternative to simple classes. You could rewrite the example above like this:

```
let iceCreamCone = (scoops:2, flavor:"chocolate", style:"cone")
println("I'd like \(iceCreamCone.scoops) scoop(s) of
➡\(iceCreamCone.flavor) in a \(iceCreamCone.style)")
//I'd like 2 scoop(s) of chocolate in a cone
```

Being able to return multiple values from a function by using tuples is a way to make your code both easier to understand and more efficient. Returning multiple values in a tuple is easy. Here's an example:

```
func numberCounts(nums: [Int]) -> (Int, Int) {
    var evenCount = 0
    var oddCount = 0
    for number in nums {
        if number % 2 == 0 {
            evenCount += 1
        }
        else {
            oddCount += 1
        }
    }
    return (evenCount, oddCount)
}
```

```
let randomNumbers = [2, 5, 14, 17, 22, 81, 96]
let counts = numberCounts(randomNumbers)
//(4, 3)
```

You can name the elements of a tuple that are returned from a function. If you change the function declaration to be:

```
func numberCounts(nums: [Int]) -> (even: Int, odd: Int)
```

then you can add clarity to the returned tuple when accessing the data:

```
let counts = numberCounts(randomNumbers)
println("We found \(counts.even) even and
➥\(counts.odd) odd numbers")
```

When a tuple contains values that you don't need, you can use an underscore (_) in that position to tell the compiler to ignore the value during decomposition:

```
let iceCreamCone = (2, "chocolate", "cone")
let (_, flavor, _) = iceCreamCone
//flavor: String = "chocolate"
```

On the surface, tuples can seem like a superficial data type because you could get the same behavior by using custom classes or Any arrays. However, tuples have many advantages over those alternatives. Tuples have specific typing that would be lost by using `Any` arrays, and you don't want to introduce potentially unsafe code when unnecessary. Also, creating custom classes that are used only for holding data adds unnecessary complexity without adding value. Due to their lightweight and flexible implementation, tuples provide a way of modeling data that is easy to use and provides a more natural way of representing certain types of data that isn't possible in languages that don't have tuples.

2.6 `switch` Statements and Pattern Matching

A lot of the syntax of Swift should look familiar to Objective-C developers. For example, on the surface, the `switch` statement works in a similar manner in Swift as it does in Objective-C. However, the `switch` statement in Swift actually provides much more power, flexibility, and safety than a `switch` statement written in a C-based language. `case` statements in a Swift `switch` statement can take advantage of pattern matching to provide much more flexibility when defining the branches of the `switch`. Also, to make `switch` statements less susceptible to errors, `case` statements don't automatically "fall through," and all possible values must be accounted for in the `case` statements. Here's an example of a simple `switch` statement:

```
func colorForIndexPath(indexPath: NSIndexPath) -> UIColor {
    var color:UIColor!
    switch (indexPath.section) {
    case 0:
        color = UIColor.redColor()
    case 1:
        color = UIColor.blueColor()
    default:
        color = UIColor.whiteColor()
    }
    return color
}
```

This example looks very similar to a `switch` statement in C. One thing to notice in this simple example, though, is that there isn't a `break` statement in the first `case`, but it is still the only `case` that is executed. This is an important difference between the behavior of a `switch` statement in Swift and a `switch` statement in C: If you want code to fall through into the next `case`, you must explicitly cause this behavior by using the `fallthrough` keyword. Here's an example of creating fallthrough behavior:

```
func colorForIndexPath(indexPath: NSIndexPath) -> UIColor {
    switch (indexPath.section) {
    case 0:
        fallthrough
    case 2:
        fallthrough
    case 4:
        return UIColor.blueColor()
    default:
        return UIColor.whiteColor()
    }
}
```

The examples so far barely scratch the surface of the power of Swift's switch statements. case statements can match values, ranges, or patterns and can also bind values, which can then be used inside the case statements. Here's an example of matching ranges:

```
let httpStatusCode = 404

switch httpStatusCode {
case 100...199:
    println("\(httpStatusCode) is an informational status")
case 200...299:
    println("\(httpStatusCode) is an success status")
case 300...399:
    println("\(httpStatusCode) is an redirection status")
case 400...499:
    println("\(httpStatusCode) is an client error status")
case 500...599:
    println("\(httpStatusCode) is an server error status")
default:
    println("\(httpStatusCode) is not a valid code")
}
```

By combining tuples with switch statements, you have a powerful flow control structure that is far more advanced than what is possible with C-style switch statements. The following example expands on what you've learned about tuples to demonstrate more advanced uses of Swift's switch statement:

```
let iceCreamCup = (scoops:2, flavor:"chocolate", style:"cup")

switch iceCreamCup {
case (0,_,_):
    println("I don't like ice cream")
case (1,"vanilla",_):
    println("One single scoop of vanilla for me")
case (1,_,_):
    println("I'd like one scoop of \(iceCreamCup.flavor) in a
➥\(iceCreamCup.style)")
case (_, "chocolate", _):
    println("I love chocolate and I want \(iceCreamCup.scoops)
➥scoops!")
default:
    println("I'd like \(iceCreamCup.scoops) scoop(s) of
➥\(iceCreamCup.flavor) in a \(iceCreamCup.style)")
}
```

Another specific use is to define a where clause to a case to provide an extra level of flexibility to switch statements. You can also bind data as part of the case matching, which helps create code that is more readable and also more compact.

The power and expressiveness of Swift switch statements goes well beyond the power and expressiveness of C-style switches. They're a good example of the philosophies of safety and expressiveness that embody Swift.

Here's an example of a switch statement that has data binding and where clauses:

```
let indexSizeAndValue = (9, 10, "")
switch indexSizeAndValue {
case (0,_, let value):
    println("The first value is \(value)")
case let (index,size, "") where index == (size-1):
    println("The last value is empty")
case let (index,size,value) where index == (size-1):
    println("The last value is \(value)")
case let (index,_,value):
    println("The value at index \(index) is \(value)")
}
```

CAUTION

When multiple patterns match on a `switch` statement, only the first `case` statement that is matched executes. Make sure to always have the more specific patterns come before general patterns when there is a possibility of matching multiple patterns.

If you look closely at each of these `case` statements, you can see how easy it is to write readable, flexible code. The first `case` statement, `case (0, _ , let value)`, matches any value where the first element of the tuple is `0`, and it also binds the third element to a new constant with the name `value` that can be used in the body of the `case` statement. Using this pattern of binding data in the `case` clause creates code that is much easier to read than assigning the values inside the `case` statement's body.

The second `case` statement, `case let (index, size, "") where index == (size-1)`, shows how to use value binding for multiple elements. Notice that the keyword `let` is before the whole tuple—and it adds an additional requirement for matching the `case` statement by using a `where` clause.

You may have noticed that there isn't a default `case` in this example. This is because the last `case`, `case let (index, _ ,value)`, matches any remaining values and fulfills the requirement of providing a comprehensive set of `case` statements. By requiring an exhaustive set of `case` statements, `switch` statements provide more safety than a series of `if/else` statements, and when combined with value binding and `where` clauses, `switch` statements provide a useful and convenient control flow mechanism.

Exercises

1. Use `String`'s `toInt()` method to create a function that adds two strings together and returns an `Int?`. Then create a function that takes an array of strings and computes a sum. Once you have a working function, can you make the code more readable by using optional binding?

2. Write a function that takes a string and an array of strings and returns the index of the string if it is found in the array or `-1` if it is not found. Next, make this function return an optional `Int`. How do these two implementations compare in terms of code readability and safety?

3. The `String` type has a `debugDescription` property. Write a function that iterates over an array of strings and prints to the console the value in `debugDescription`. Next, extend this function by using generics. How much of the function's body did you have to change? Did you have to change how the function is called when using a `[String]`?

4. Some types can be implicitly converted to other types. Add a float type declaration to the variable `myNumber`:

   ```
   var myNumber = 2
   var myDivisionResult = 7 / myNumber
   ```

   How does the behavior of this variable change?

5. Several methods on standard objects in Swift take closures as parameters. Use the `sort` method on an array with a closure that sorts an array of `Int` from largest to smallest.

6. Nested functions can be returned and then executed in the calling scope. Make a function that takes a string and returns a function that doesn't take any parameters and returns a string. (This string should be a string that is created using the original argument and modified in the nested function.) Here's what the function signature should look like:

   ```
   func stringCreator(initialString:String) -> (() -> String)
   ```

7. Write a function that takes a tuple that represents an x and y coordinate and returns the two-dimensional Cartesian quadrant that contains the coordinate. Next, modify the function to return a tuple that contains named values for x, y, and the quadrant.

8. Write a generic function that takes an array of objects and returns an array of tuples that combine the elements into pairs. (Objects at indexes 0 and 1 would be the first tuple.) How could you handle an array with an odd number of elements?

9. Take a series of `if/else` statements from an existing project and convert it to a `switch` statement in Swift. Is the code more readable? Were you able to reduce the number of lines of code? Is the Swift code safer?

10. Given a tuple that represents a three-dimensional point (x, y, z), write a `switch` statement that prints out the point's octant (or the origin). Next, extend this `switch` statement to match cases where two of the values within the point are equal. Can you rewrite your `switch` to use value binding or underscores in the pattern matching to make the code more readable?

3

Objects and Classes

Topics in This Chapter

In Chapter 1, "Introducing Swift," you saw that structs and enums in Swift are more powerful than their counterparts in C-based languages, and they are more akin to classes. All three data structure types are first-class types in Swift and can have properties, type methods, and instance methods, and developers can extend them as needed. This chapter goes into detail about the various types, their differences, and why you would use one type over another.

These are the key points in this chapter:

- Enumerations and structures in Swift are very much like classes and can include type and instance properties and methods.

- Enumerations and structures are value types, which means they're copied as they're passed around in code; on the other hand, classes are reference types, which means a reference to an object is passed around in code.

- Enumerations, structures, and classes may have methods (including their `init()` methods) overloaded to accept different sets of arguments.

- Classes may be subclassed, with some rules set in place by the parent class, such as marking methods as `final` to prevent them from being overridden and marking `init()` methods as `required` to ensure that subclasses include them.

- When overriding a method in a subclass, you must confirm to the compiler that you intend to do so by using the `override` keyword.

- A subclass that provides its own designated `init()` methods does not inherit the `init()` methods from its parent class.

- Properties may be stored or computed and may have observers attached to them to execute a closure before and/or after a property is updated.

- Custom classes may make subscripting syntax available to developers to provide easy access to internal data.

- A protocol defines a set of properties and/or methods that a type must contain in order to conform to that protocol.

- Protocols are a type unto themselves and can be used as the type required for a parameter or as a return type.

- Enumerations, structures, and classes may be extended through extensions, with the ability to add computed properties and/or methods—even for types that do not make their source code available.

- You can use access control to hide implementation details in your classes or to make specific entities public and available to other modules.

3.1 Enumerations

You can use an enumeration to create a custom data type with a predefined set of possible values. For example, you could create a NetworkConnection type that could be either NotConnected, WiFi, or Cellular. Here's how you'd do it:

```
enum NetworkConnection {
    case NotConnected
    case WiFi
    case Cellular
}
```

Then you can create a variable in your app to monitor your current connection and update it as the connection changes:

```
var currentConnection = NetworkConnection.WiFi
```

Here currentConnection is inferred to be of type NetworkConnection because you're initializing it to a NetworkConnection type as you declare it. Because the compiler knows what type currentConnection is, you can update its value by using a shorter dot notation omitting the type:

```
currentConnection = .Cellular
```

You can use the variable in a switch construct in order to update the app's interface for the current connection:

```
switch currentConnection {
case .NotConnected:
    showOfflineIndicator()
case .WiFi:
    showWiFiIndicator()
case .Cellular:
    showCellularIndicator()
}
```

By default, an enum in Swift does not map its members to a basic Int type, as you might expect if you're used to that behavior in C-based languages. So members of an enumeration in Swift have no defined order unless explicitly set. NotConnected is not less than WiFi; they are only not equal to each other. Instead, the possible members are their own value and can only be checked for equality to other members in the same enum. Here's how it looks:

```
//check for equality to a possible NetworkConnection member
if currentConnection == NetworkConnection.WiFi {
    //we're connected to a WiFi

}


if currentConnection > NetworkConnection.NotConnected {
    //error: we cannot check if one member is greater than or
    //less than another member as they have no order

}
```

If your type should have a defined order, you can change the `enum` to use another type as its raw type and assign a raw value to each member:

```
enum NetworkConnection: Int {
    case NotConnected = 0
    case WiFi = 1
    case Cellular = 2

}
```

Now the `NetworkConnection` type is backed by the `Int` type, and each member is assigned a unique raw value. The example above specifies a value for each member, but you could omit them and let the compiler automatically assign values to the other members by just incrementing the starting value. Now you can use the raw values for comparisons, just as you would with any `Int` variables, by accessing the `rawValue` property on the member:

```
if currentConnection.rawValue >
➥NetworkConnection.NotConnected.rawValue {
    //we have a connection, it could be WiFi or Cellular

}
```

You can also associate values with members in an `enum`. For example, you can redeclare `NetworkConnection` to include additional information about the connection:

```
enum NetworkConnection {
    case NotConnected
    case WiFi(String, Int)
    case Cellular(Int)

}
```

If the app is not connected, there's no other information you need. If the app is connected via a Wi-Fi connection, you can store the network name as well as the ping time to the server. When the app is connected via the cellular network, you can just store the ping time:

```
let networkName: String = getNetworkName()
let pingTime: Int = calculatePingTime()
currentConnection = .WiFi(networkName, pingTime)
```

Whenever you detect a change in the network status, you update the variable. In this case the app has switched to a cellular connection:

```
let pingTime: Int = calculatePingTime()
currentConnection = .Cellular(pingTime)
```

The variable currentConnection can only ever be equal to one of the members at a time. When you're changing from one value to another, the values associated with the previous setting are lost because they are no longer relevant.

To access the associated values, you expand the switch from earlier:

```
switch currentConnection {
case .NotConnected:
    println("Not Connected")
    showOfflineIndicator()
case .WiFi(let networkName, let pingTime):
    println("WiFi [\(networkName): \(pingTime)ms]")
    showWiFiIndicator()
case .Cellular(let pingTime):
    println("Cellular [\(pingTime)ms]")
    showCellularIndicator()
}
```

You can expand an enum in Swift to include both type methods (using the static keyword) and instance methods. Here's how you can add an instance method to return a helpful description of the current value of a NetworkConnection instance:

```
enum NetworkConnection {
    case NotConnected
    case WiFi(String, Int)
    case Cellular(Int)
```

```
    func description() -> String {
        switch self {
        case .NotConnected:
            return "Not Connected"
        case .WiFi(let networkName, let pingTime):
            return "WiFi [\(networkName): \(pingTime)ms]"
        case .Cellular(let pingTime):
            return "Cellular [\(pingTime)ms]"
        }
    }
}


currentConnection = .WiFi("Home", 34)
println("Connection -> \(currentConnection.description())")
//output: Connection -> WiFi [Home: 34ms]
```

If a method will alter the value of the instance, it must indicate this to the compiler by prefacing the method declaration with the `mutating` keyword. This lets the compiler know that the method cannot be called on constant instances—those declared using the `let` keyword:

```
enum NetworkConnection {
    case NotConnected
    case WiFi(String, Int)
    case Cellular(Int)

    func description() -> String {
        switch self {
        case .NotConnected:
            return "Not Connected"
        case .WiFi(let networkName, let pingTime):
            return "WiFi [\(networkName): \(pingTime)ms]"
        case .Cellular(let pingTime):
            return "Cellular [\(pingTime)ms]"
        }
    }
```

```
    mutating func lostConnection() {
        self = .NotConnected
    }
}
```

3.2 Classes

A class in Swift is just what you expect if you come from almost any other object-oriented language. Each class combines a set of related variables and functions into a cohesive unit in order to reduce the overall complexity of the app. Classes can inherit behavior from other classes, conform to protocols, or be extended by way of extensions. A class can be instantiated into an object (an instance) that will encompass a specific unit of data and represent something in your app, such as a specific view or data record.

Some functions in a class are called on the class itself; these are type methods (also known as class methods). Other functions are called on an instance of the class; these are instance methods, and they generally affect only the specific instance they are called on. Classes are reference types, so when you pass instances of a class around in your code, you're passing a reference to an object, not duplicating it.

Here is a sample class that shows the basic usage:

```
class Device {
    //MARK: Properties
    let type: String
    let identifier: String
    var name: String
    let totalCapacity = 0
    var freeCapacity = 0
    let hasCellular = false

    //MARK: Initializers
    init(type: String, identifier: String, name: String,
    ➡totalCapacity: Int, systemUsage: Int) {
        //Part 1 - Initialize all properties
        self.type = type
        self.identifier = identifier
        self.name = name
```

```
        self.totalCapacity = totalCapacity
        freeCapacity = self.totalCapacity - systemUsage


        //Part 2 - Can access self.methods
        saveToDatabase()
    }


    //MARK: De-initializers
    deinit {
        //Clean up here before the instance is destroyed
    }


    //MARK: Class Methods
    class func findDeviceWithIdentifier(identifier: String)
-> Device? {
        //TODO: look up device in the database
        return nil
    }


    //MARK: Instance Methods
    func saveToDatabase() -> Bool {
        //TODO: implement this
        return true
    }
}
```

Let's go through this example a section at a time. Notice that the `class` keyword indicates that you're defining a class, and everything inside the main set of braces is part of that class. This sample class does not inherit from any other class, nor does it conform to any protocols. (We'll cover those possibilities later in the chapter.)

The first section in this class contains the properties. Some of them are constants, and some are variables, depending on how you plan to use them in the app. For some of these properties you assign a default value, and for others you don't. Before you can use an instance of this class, you must initialize every property. Those that have a default value set are automatically initialized. For the others, you must set an initial value in one of the `init()` functions.

NOTE

In Swift classes, there is just one variable for each property. In Objective-C, there is the property, and there is an instance variable (`ivar`) backing up that property; you could encounter different results, depending on how you accessed the variable. Using `self.property` would actually call the `getter` or `setter` method for that property, which would often, but not always, access the value of the related `ivar`. Sometimes, however, the `getter` or `setter` method would perform some calculation or make other method calls before accessing the `ivar`, and it could even ignore the `ivar` altogether. Using `property` (or perhaps `_property`) alone, without the `self.` prefix, would access the `ivar` directly, bypassing the `getter` or `setter` method. This has led to a lot of bugs and is something that cannot happen in Swift because accessing a property as `self.property` or simply `property` has exactly the same effect. The only time you need to actually specify the `self.` prefix is when there is a second local variable in the method with the same name, as is often the case inside the `init()` methods, as you'll see next.

In this class, you have just one `init()` function, and it takes five parameters that it uses to initialize the properties. As mentioned earlier, you must initialize all the properties before you can use the class—even inside the `init()` functions. An `init()` function effectively has two parts:

- In the first part, you handle the initialization of properties.

- In the second part, you can trigger other methods in the class for additional setup.

This means you cannot call another method in the class in order to get a value and use it for the initialization. If you need to do something like that, you need to use a default value or set an initial value in the first part of the `init()`, and then you can perform the calculation in the second part and assign the result to your property at that point. The compiler enforces this, and you'll receive a compile-time error if you try to access `self` (except to differentiate between a parameter and a property) in an `init()` method before initializing all the properties or if the `init()` returns before the initialization is complete.

In the `init()` method above, the first four parameter names are exactly equal to property names of this class. This naming is good practice because it makes the code easy to read. Because the parameter has the smallest scope (available only in that method), it shadows the property with the same name. In order to access the property, you need to include the `self.` prefix here. Because there is no duplication for the `freeCapacity` property, you can access it directly and omit the `self.` prefix. The example above also has a property called `hasCellular` that isn't set in the `init()` method, because it's declared with a default value that is sufficient and meets the initialization obligations.

 NOTE

If you look at the previous code carefully, you might see that it's doing something a little odd. Some of the properties have been declared as constants, with the `let` keyword, yet the example assigns them values. This might look okay for the `type` and `identifier` properties because they need to be initialized, but the `totalCapacity` property is set to a default of `0`, and yet the example sets a new value. `init()` methods have special powers in that they can set and/or change constant properties for their own instance, even multiple times in the same `init()` method. The constant properties aren't locked until the `init()` returns or completes.

Once everything has been initialized, you're free to reference `self` and call the `saveToDatabase()` method. (The `self.` prefix is implied on the method call.)

The next section in the class is for `deinit`, the de-initializer for the class; notice that it is not a function, nor does it have parentheses. This is the `dealloc` equivalent in Swift, and it gives you a last chance to clean up anything you need to clean up before the instance is destroyed. Some common tasks you would handle in the `deinit` are the following:

- Free any resources that wouldn't be handled by ARC

- Remove the instance from any observers, Notification Center, or KVO

- Close any files or streams that may be open

- Clear any delegates

In the simple class example above, you don't actually need to do anything in the `deinit`, and you could safely omit it.

Next in the sample class is a type method. The keyword `class` precedes the `func` keyword to indicate that this is a class method—a function that is called on the class directly, not an instance of the class. The function `findDeviceWithIdentifier()` takes one parameter, `identifier` of type `String`, and returns an optional `Device`. The implementation of the function has been omitted, but the idea is that it would search the database for a device record that matches the `identifier`, and it would return an instance of the `Device` class that represents the indicated record. If no matching device were found, `nil` would be returned.

In practice, the `findDeviceWithIdentifier()` class method would be called like this:

```
if let myDevice = Device.findDeviceWithIdentifier("ABCD1234") {
    println("Found a matching device: \(myDevice.name)")
}
else {
    println("No matching device found")
}
```

The final part of the sample class is an instance method named `saveToDatabase()`. Again, the example above skips the implementation, but the declaration shows that it takes no parameters, and it returns a Boolean to indicate whether the save was successful. Because this is an instance method, you would call this on a specific instance of `Device`, like so:

```
var newDevice = Device(type: "phone", identifier: "ABCD1234",
➥name: "My Phone", totalCapacity: 16*1024*1024, systemUsage:
➥2*1024*1024)

newDevice.saveToDatabase()
```

 NOTE

The order of the items inside your class definition does not matter. You can mix up properties, methods, class methods, initializers, and the de-initializer, and you can scramble them as you see fit. It makes sense to use some sort of logical order, though, so that future readers of your code can quickly find what they're looking for. This usually means grouping similar items together, such as grouping all the properties together, grouping all the `init()` functions together, grouping all the methods of a protocol together, and so on.

3.3 Structures

In Swift, a structure shares almost all the details of a class that we just covered in the preceding section. These are the key differences:

- You use the `struct` keyword rather than the `class` keyword to declare a structure.

- A structure cannot inherit from another structure (or class), although it can conform to protocols or be extended.

- If you don't declare an `init()` method, a default memberwise `init()` method will be automatically created for you.

- There is no `deinit` available for a structure.

- A type method is a `static` method in a structure.

- A structure may have static properties, while a class cannot (at least not directly, but see a workaround in Chapter 8, "Common Patterns").

- Structures are value types, so when you pass them around in your code, you're making new copies.

- When a method on a `struct` will change a value in the `struct`, the method must be marked as `mutating`, as shown for enumerations.

Here's a simple structure:

```
struct PointOfInterest {
    var x: Float
    var y: Float
    var name: String
}
```

This structure has three variable properties:

- Two floats for the coordinates

- A string to name the point

Because this example does not include an `init()` method, the compiler automatically supplies a memberwise `init()` method for you. It takes a parameter for each property, and uses the equivalent name. It is as if you've included this `init()` method yourself:

```
init(x: Float, y: Float, name: String) {
    self.x = x
    self.y = y
    self.name = name
}
```

You can create an instance of this structure like so:

```
var myHouse = PointOfInterest(x: 5, y: 10, name: "My House")
```

If you provide your own `init()` method, the automatic memberwise method is not created for you anymore.

NOTE

A common problem in Objective-C occurs when you use a structure as a property of a class. In Objective-C, you cannot update a property of a structure property directly because of the way `getters` work. You will often see this pattern:

```
CGRect frame = view.frame;

frame.size.width += 50;

view.frame = frame;
```

What's happening here is that you're extracting the whole structure into a temporary variable, making changes to its properties, and then assigning the whole structure back. In Swift, this problem no longer exists, and you can directly access properties of properties:

```
view.frame.size.width += 50
```

 NOTE

Because classes and structures are so similar, it may not be obvious when you should use one over the other. The most important factor is the *by value* or *by reference* effect when passing instances around in your code. If the object is small and simple enough (that is, no classes as properties), then copying the object each time it's passed somewhere may be okay, or even desired, so a `struct` may be a good fit. If the object has a `class` as a property, that property will be passed by reference even if the containing object is a `struct` that's copied. This will produce some odd behavior, so you should use a `class` as the containing object.

If you want the object to respond to notifications, it will have to be a `class`, since adding a `struct` to Notification Center will actually add a copy of the `struct`, and the wrong structure will receive the notifications.

Finally, structures cannot inherit, so if you need to inherit behavior from a parent object, you must use a `class`.

3.4 Subclassing

A `class` in Swift is able to inherit from one other `class`, just as is possible in Objective-C. The new `class` is a child of the original parent class and inherits the behavior of that parent class, but it can have additional behaviors added. You indicate that the child class inherits from the parent class by appending a colon and the parent class name to the new class name:

```
class Record {
    var primaryId: Int = 0

    func save() -> Bool {
        //TODO: add implementation
        return true
    }
}

class Item: Record {
    var name: String = ""
}

var myItem = Item()
myItem.primaryId = 3
//sets the primaryId property inherited from the Record class
myItem.name = "Socks"
//sets the name property in the Item class
myItem.save()
//calls the save() method inherited from the Record class
```

3.5 Overloading

Overloading is when two or more methods in a single object share the same name but have a different set of arguments. When you later call the method by name on an object, the compiler automatically uses the version of the method that matches the parameters you've supplied. Classes, structures, and enumerations in Swift are all able to overload their methods.

The following is a simple example of a `class` with overloaded methods:

```
class Account {
    var balance:Float = 0

    //deposit(): takes a single Float as a parameter
    func deposit(amount: Float) {
        println("Depositing single item: $\(amount)")
```

```
        balance += amount

    }


    //deposit(): takes an array of Floats as a parameter
    func deposit(funds: [Float]) {
        println("Depositing \(funds.count) item(s)")
        for amount in funds {
            println(" -> $\(amount)")
            balance += amount
        }
    }
}
```

This simple `Account` class tracks the balance of a bank account. There are two functions named `deposit()`. The first one takes a `Float` parameter, and the second takes an array of `Floats` for depositing multiple items at the same time.

Here's the `Account` class in use:

```
var myAccount = Account()
myAccount.deposit(50.0)
//output: Depositing single item: $50.0


myAccount.deposit([100.0, 50.0, 200.0])
//output: Depositing 3 item(s)
//output:    -> $100.0
//output:    -> $50.0
//output:    -> $200.0
```

You can see from the output that the correct method was called in each case. When overloading, you must ensure that each version of the method takes a different set of arguments, by type. As long as the number of arguments and/or the type of arguments changes for each version, the compiler can differentiate and use the correct one. A subclass may add additional overloaded methods.

 NOTE

This example uses different log messages to show the difference between the two `deposit()` implementations. In real-world usage, the second implementation would call the first implementation for each value in the `funds` array.

3.6 Overriding

When a class inherits from another class, it's possible that the child class will duplicate a function that's already provided in the parent class. If the parameters are slightly different, the new function will overload the original, as you've just seen. If the parameters are exactly the same, the compiler treats this as a possible programmer mistake and gives you a compile-time error. This prevents you from accidentally overriding a parent's method that you may or may not have known exists.

If you want to override the parent method, you must explicitly tell the compiler so by prefacing the function with the `override` keyword. When defining the parent class, you can prevent a subclass from overriding a method by prefacing the function with the `final` keyword. Whenever a method is overridden, the parent's version of that method is then hidden and unavailable outside the child class. The child can still access the original version of the method, if needed, by calling `super.method()`:

```
class Record {
    var primaryId: Int = 0

    final func save() -> Bool {
        println("Record.save()")
        //TODO: add implementation
        return true
    }

    func delete() -> Bool {
        println("Record.delete()")
        //TODO: add implementation
        return true
    }
}


class Item : Record {
    var name: String = ""

    override func delete() -> Bool {
        println("Item.delete()")
        if (!safeToDelete()) {
            println("Unable to delete: \(name)")
```

```
        return false
    }


    return super.delete()
}


func safeToDelete() -> Bool {
    //TODO: add implementation
    return true
}
}
```

In this example, the `save()` function is marked `final` to prevent subclasses from altering the way the record is saved. The `Item` class overrides the `delete()` function in order to add a check on whether it is safe to delete this item. If it is deemed unsafe, the item's `delete()` function will fail and return `false`. However, if it is safe to delete, the code calls the parent's `delete()` function and allows it to carry out its implementation.

3.7 Initialization

You've seen that when creating a class, you must initialize all its properties before you can actually use an instance. You accomplish this by either providing a default value for each property or using an `init()` method to initialize the values, perhaps based on parameters passed to the `init()` function. You've also seen that you can overload methods by providing multiple methods that share a name but have different parameter lists. You can combine these techniques and overload the `init()` function, thereby providing multiple ways to create a new instance of a class.

Here's a simple example:

```
class ShoppingCart {
    var items: [String]

    init() {
        items = [String]()
    }


    init(item: String) {
```

```
        items = [String]()
        items.append(item)
    }
}


var cart1 = ShoppingCart()
//cart1 is initialized with the first init() method,
//cart1 contains no items
var cart2 = ShoppingCart(item: "Model X")
//cart2 is initialized with the second init() method,
//cart2 contains 1 item
```

This example shows a class with two possible `init()` methods, each able to fully initialize the object. There is a problem with this example, though. The second `init()` method duplicates the code of the first `init()` method, giving twice as much code to maintain in the future. The solution is to have the second `init()` method call the first one so that the bulk of the initialization is done in one common place. When you do that, the second `init()` method is no longer able to fully initialize the object on its own because it relies on the first. It becomes a convenient way to initialize the object and add the first item to the cart.

In Swift, you differentiate between two types of `init()` methods:

- An `init()` method that is able to fully initialize the object is called a *designated initializer.*

- An `init()` method that relies on another to complete the initialization is called a *convenience initializer.*

You identify a convenience initializer by prefacing the declaration with the `convenience` keyword:

```
class ShoppingCart {
    var items: [String]

    init() {
        items = [String]()
    }
```

```
convenience init(item: String) {
    self.init()
    items.append(item)
}
}
```

Initialization is complicated slightly when inheritance comes into play. When a class inherits from a parent class, it may or may not inherit the `init()` methods. If the new class provides its own designated initializer method, it will not inherit any of the superclass's `init()` methods. If the new class provides only additional convenience `init()` methods or no additional `init()` methods, it will inherit all the `init()` methods from the parent. These are some of Swift's safety features. The idea is that if a child class provides a designated initializer, it likely initializes properties that aren't in the parent class, or it does some other setup that is not handled in the parent's designated initializers, so the parent's initializers are incomplete and will no longer work correctly. Thus they are not included in the subclass in order to prevent a programmer from accidentally using them. If your class needs a specific `init()` to exist in subclasses, you can designate that by prefacing the `init()` method with the keyword `required`, and the compiler will enforce that requirement for you.

In Section 3.2, "Classes," we explain that an `init()` method is actually a two-part process, and you must ensure that all properties are initialized before you call other methods in the class. This applies equally in the designated and convenience `init()` methods, but it may seem a little backward. If your `init()` method will be calling another `init()` method in the same class, it must do so before setting any properties itself; otherwise, its values may be overridden by the other `init()`. If the `init()` method will be calling an `init()` in a superclass, it must initialize its own properties first.

3.8 Properties

Properties come in a variety of types in Swift. The most common type is a stored property, with a variable attached to an instance of a class. You've seen this in the examples above, simply declared with `var` or `let` (for constants), and assigned either a default value or initialized to some value when the object is instantiated.

Another common type of property is a computed property. Computed properties do not have an associated variable and thus do not directly store any data. They are used to access or calculate (and optionally set) other data indirectly in a class. In Objective-C, all properties are essentially computed properties, but you could make them act like stored properties by using an associated `ivar` for storage.

When you (or the compiler, if this is done automatically) synthesize a property, you provide a `getter` and a `setter` method that either accesses or updates the related `ivar` or performs some other calculation in order to produce the value needed. It would look something like this:

```
//Crate.h
@interface Crate : NSObject   {
    NSString* _name;
    NSInteger _grams;
}


@property (nonatomic, strong, getter=name, setter=setName:)
➡NSString* name;
@property (nonatomic, assign, getter=grams, setter=setGrams:)
➡NSInteger grams;


@end


//Crate.m
@implementation Crate


@synthesize name = _name;
@synthesize grams = _grams;


- (NSString*)name {
    return _name;
}


- (void)setName:(NSString*)name {
    _name = name;
}


- (NSInteger)grams {
    return _grams;
}
```

```
- (void) setGrams: (NSInteger) grams {

    _grams = grams;

}
```

```
@end
```

This example is a little drawn out because modern Objective-C will handle a lot of this for you automatically. But even if it's generated automatically, it's all there, and this example shows what's really happening. Each time you access a property in Objective-C, you're really calling the getter method, which then returns the value stored in the backing variable. To set that same property, you actually pass the value you want to the setter method, which updates the backing variable. In both cases, you don't really have direct access to the backing variable; it's really smoke and mirrors simulating properties behind the scenes. Interestingly, Objective-C didn't even have these simulated properties until version 2.0; you had to call the getter and setter methods directly, like this:

```
[myCrate setName:@"Apples"];
```

```
NSLog(@"I have a crate of %@", [myCrate name]);
```

NOTE

In Objective-C, when declaring a property, you set that property as either nonatomic or atomic (the default, if you don't specify). In Swift, all properties are nonatomic; there is no option for atomic.

This same class in Swift would look like this:

```
class Crate {

    var name: String? = nil

    var grams = 0

}
```

In Swift, you actually have direct access to the variables. There isn't a getter or setter working behind the scenes. Instead, you have straightforward stored properties.

3.8.1 Computed Properties

You can use a computed property by declaring a getter and optionally a setter:

```
class Crate {

    var name: String? = nil

    var grams = 0
```

```
    var lbs: Float {
        get {
            return Float(grams) / 454
        }
        set(newValue) {
            grams = Int(newValue * 454)
        }
    }
}
```

This example includes a computed property called `lbs` that calculates the weight of the crate based on the `grams` property. Because you add a `setter`, you can specify the weight of the crate in pounds, and you're actually updating the `grams` property. If you omit the entire set closure, `lbs` will be a read-only property.

Here's the property in action:

```
var myCrate = Crate()
myCrate.grams = 1135
println("myCrate weighs \(myCrate.lbs) lbs")
//output: myCrate weighs 2.5 lbs
//Someone eats an apple that weighs about 1/3 of a pound
myCrate.lbs -= 0.3
println("myCrate weighs now weighs \(myCrate.grams) g")
//output: myCrate weighs 998 g
```

3.8.2 Property Observers

Swift gives you a convenient way to add observers to properties. By using the same syntax as with `getters` and `setters`, described earlier, you can add closures for `willSet` and `didSet` to execute code just before or just after the property is updated. Here's an example that expands on the `Crate` class and adds some tracking info:

```
class Crate {
    var name: String? = nil
    var destination: String? = nil
    var grams = 0
    var lbs: Float {
        get {
            return Float(grams) / 454
```

```
        }
        set(newValue) {
            grams = Int(newValue * 454)
        }
    }


    var trackedLocations: [String] = [String]() {
        willSet(newValue) {
            if trackedLocations.isEmpty {
                println("Starting in \(newValue[0])")
            }
        }


        didSet(oldValue) {
            if let unwrappedDestination = destination {
                if trackedLocations[trackedLocations.count
- 1] == unwrappedDestination {
                    println("Arrived: \(unwrappedDestination)")
                }
            }
        }
    }
}


var myCrate = Crate()
myCrate.destination = "Cupertino"
myCrate.trackedLocations.append("Toronto")
//output: Starting in Toronto
myCrate.trackedLocations.append("Denver")
myCrate.trackedLocations.append("Los Angeles")
myCrate.trackedLocations.append("Cupertino")
//output: Arrived: Cupertino
println("Locations: \(myCrate.trackedLocations)")
//output: Locations: [Toronto, Denver, Los Angeles, Cupertino]
```

This example adds the trackedLocations array of strings to track locations as
the package travels around the world. A willSet closure tests the array before you
update it to see if it's empty. If so, it means you're adding the first location, and

you can alert the customer that the crate is on its way. After the location has been added to the array, a `didSet` closure checks to see if the package has arrived at its final destination. If so, you alert the customer that the package has arrived.

Something interesting to note in this example is that it doesn't actually set the `trackedLocations` property. The array is set during the initialization of the object, after which you only append values to that same array. Swift's `willSet` and `didSet` observers trigger any time the property or its properties are altered.

 NOTE

The `set`, `willSet`, and `didSet` closures above include a parameter. You have the option to rename the parameter to something more descriptive or omit it altogether and use the default parameter name (that is used explicitly here).

3.8.3 `lazy` Properties

You already know that when an object is instantiated, all its properties must be initialized, either with a default value or by having a value assigned in its `init()` method. In some cases, this may be an expensive or impossible task. A property may be of a type that takes some time to initialize; it could rely on disk I/O or database access, or it could require a network call in order to complete. It's also possible that after doing the work needed to initialize it, the app may release the object for another reason, and that expensive property will not have been used. That would be a lot of work for nothing. For such cases, Swift includes the `lazy` keyword. If you flag a property by prefacing the definition with the `lazy` keyword, the compiler will drop the requirement that it be initialized and defer the initialization until the property is first used. Here's what this looks like:

```
class Company {
    var name: String? = nil
    lazy var logo: UIImage = self.downloadLogo()


    func downloadLogo() -> UIImage {
        //TODO: add implementation
        return UIImage()
    }
}
```

Now you can quickly instantiate a bunch of `Company` objects, and the downloading of their logo images will be deferred until you attempt to display the image.

This example uses the method `downloadLogo()`, but you could supply a closure, which won't be executed until the property is accessed:

```
lazy var logo: UIImage = {
    //TODO: add implementation
    return UIImage()
} ()
```

Notice the parentheses after the closure.

3.9 Subscripting

Using subscripts is a quick and easy way to access a portion of a data structure. You use them with arrays all the time (for example, `myArray[3] = "something"`) and with dictionaries (for example, `myDictionary["firstName"] = "Elon"`). Swift allows you to use subscripts with your own classes, structures, and enumerations.

To add subscripting to objects, you add special closures named `subscript`, using syntax that's a hybrid of the syntax for properties and methods. The following example creates a basic implementation of a 3D game board—a 100×100×100 matrix. There is a basic `GamePiece` class that currently holds just the game piece name but represents units in the game. These are placed throughout the board, using subscripting for the coordinates:

```
class GamePiece {
    var name: String

    init(name: String) {
        self.name = name
    }

    //TODO: add implementation
}

class SpaceTimeContinuum {
    var universeSize: Int
    var boardSpaces = [String:GamePiece]()
```

```
        init(universeSize: Int = 10) {
            self.universeSize = universeSize
        }


        func boardSpaceKeyFor(x: Int, y: Int, z: Int) -> String {
            return String(format: "%d_%d_%d", x, y, z)
        }


        subscript(x: Int, y: Int, z: Int) -> GamePiece? {
            get {
                if (x > universeSize
                    || y > universeSize
                    || z > universeSize) {
                    //Out of bounds
                    return nil
                }
                return boardSpaces[boardSpaceKeyFor(x, y: y, z: z)]
            }


            set(newValue) {
                if (x > universeSize
                    || y > universeSize
                    || z > universeSize) {
                    //Out of bounds
                    return
                }
                boardSpaces[boardSpaceKeyFor(x, y: y, z: z)]
➥= newValue
            }
        }
    }


var gameBoard = SpaceTimeContinuum(universeSize: 100)
gameBoard[0, 0, 0] = GamePiece(name: "Player 1 Ship")
gameBoard[99, 99, 99] = GamePiece(name: "Player 2 Ship")
for (var i=1; i<8; ++i) {
    gameBoard[i * 10, i * 10, i * 10] = GamePiece(name: "NPC")
}
```

```
if let piece = gameBoard[50, 50, 50] {
    println("Piece: \(piece.name)")
}
else {
    println("No piece found")
}
```

The subscript getter returns an optional GamePiece, so you don't need to worry about checking whether a piece actually exists on the board in the subscript closures. You do the check for a valid GamePiece after retrieval.

Although this example doesn't show it, it's possible to overload subscripts. Perhaps you could add a version that takes four Ints, the fourth being the turn number of the game, so you can move through the history of a completed game.

3.10 Protocols

As in Objective-C, in Swift a protocol lets you define a set of properties and/or methods that a class, a structure, or an enumeration can conform to. The protocol itself doesn't actually provide an implementation. It only defines what the implementation must look like. Here's an example protocol definition:

```
protocol Compressible {
    class var isHardwareAcceleratedCompression: Bool { get }
    var estimatedCompressionRatio: Float { get }
    var shouldCompress: Bool { get set }


    class func compressibleFormats() -> String
    func compress() -> Bool
}
```

This example creates a Compressible protocol that you can use when creating other classes, structures, and enumerations to save space when writing to disk. This protocol starts with a read-only type property named isHardwareAcceleratedCompression. You indicate that it's a type property by using the class keyword, although in a structure or an enumeration implementation of this protocol, you would use the keyword static.

As part of the property declaration, you indicate that the property must be read-write by including { get set } or that the property may be read-only with just a { get } requirement. estimatedCompressionRatio is a read-only instance property, and shouldCompress is a read-write instance property. If you look at the methods that must be supplied in order to conform to this property, you see that the class method compressibleFormats() must return a String value to indicate which compression methods are supported by the class. And the instance method compress() will perform the actual compression of the object and return a Boolean to indicate success or failure.

When you declare a class, you list the protocols it will conform after the class's parent type, like this:

```
class Image : File, Compressible {
    //TODO: add implementation
}
```

This is an Image class that inherits from the File class and conforms to the Compressible protocol. The implementation of the Image class must include all the properties and methods outlined in the protocol declaration. When you declare that an object conforms to a protocol, you are promising that all the properties and/or methods in that protocol will be available. If any are missing, you'll receive compile-time errors.

In Swift, a protocol is a complete type by itself. While this doesn't mean you can instantiate an object from a protocol (since it would have no implementation), it does mean you can specify a protocol as the type for parameters and return values, which lets you pass in any object type or return any object type, as long as it conforms to that protocol. Here's an example of a function that requires a Compressible parameter:

```
func compress(file: Compressible) -> Bool {
    //TODO: add implementation
    return true
}


var myImage: Image = Image()
compress(myImage)
```

This compress function can take any object that's Compressible, do its thing, and return a Boolean to indicate success or failure. Since myImage is of type Image, which conforms to Compressible, it's an acceptable parameter, and the compress function can safely call any of the methods the protocol promises will exist.

Protocols may also inherit from other protocols, just as classes do, and you use the same syntax. Another option is to create a protocol collection, which lets you specify that a parameter must conform to multiple protocols. Here's what it looks like:

```
protocol Savable {
    func save() -> Bool
}


func save(file: protocol<Savable, Compressible>, path:
➥String) -> Bool {
    //TODO: add implementation
    return true
}
```

The `save` function accepts a parameter called `file` that must be both `Savable` and `Compressible`. If a variable does not conform to both protocols, it is not acceptable as a parameter and will generate a compile-time error if you try to use it.

3.11 Extensions

Extensions in Swift are similar to categories in Objective-C: They enable you to add functionality to existing classes, structures, and enumerations. Extensions are extremely useful when you don't have access to, or are unable to add to, the original source. You don't have access to the source code for the basic Swift types, such as `String`, `Int`, `Double`, and so on, so you use extensions to add useful functionality.

By using extensions, you can do the following:

- Add computed properties

- Add new type and/or instance methods

- Add additional convenience initializers

- Add subscript access

- Make an existing type conform to a protocol

- Add nested types (see Chapter 8)

- Override existing methods or properties

You can't use extensions to do any of the following:

- Add stored properties

- Add designated initializers

- Add a `deinit` closure

You declare an extension by using syntax similar to that of a class:

```
protocol Reversible {
    mutating func reverse() -> String
}


extension String: Reversible {
    mutating func reverse() -> String {
        var newString = ""
        for character in self {
            newString = String(character) + newString
        }

        self = newString
        return self
    }
}
```

This example creates the protocol `Reversible` as a simple example, and then it creates an extension on `String` that conforms to the new protocol. In this case, the one method `reverse()` iterates through each `Character` in the string and builds a new string, using those characters in reverse order. Because you're going to update the value of `self` to this new string, you must declare the `reverse()` function as `mutating`. Once the new string has been constructed, you assign it to `self` to update the initial value, and then you return `self` so the function can be used in chains.

3.12 Access Control

Every type, class, structure, enumeration, constant, variable, property, function, and method (collectively grouped together as *entities*) has an access control level assigned. If the developer doesn't specify this level, the compiler applies a default level. Which level is the default depends on several factors, discussed shortly.

The Swift team has taken an approach that tries to prevent access control from getting in the way or overcomplicating things. For the most part, if you're just developing apps, you don't need to worry about access control at all and can just let the compiler set reasonable defaults. However, if you're developing a module or framework, or if you're breaking an app into multiple modules, then you'll need to pay attention to the access control settings.

Swift uses three levels of control:

- **public**: This is the highest, most accessible level. Any entity marked as public can be used by any file in the same module or by any file in any module that imports the module. This level is intended for designating which entities in code are part of an API. If you're developing a framework for others to use in their apps, you add these entities so the users can interact with your framework.

- **internal**: This is the default level unless other factors force a different default. internal entities are available to any source file in the module. If you ignore access control in an app, the compiler will likely mark everything as internal, and because all your source files will be part of the same default module, everything will be available to everything else.

- **private**: This is the lowest, least accessible level. private entities are available only to the source file they're defined in. You use this level to hide specific implementation details.

When deciding what access level any given entity should be, the general rule is that no entity can be more accessible than the types it exposes. For example, a public class cannot have a public property of a type that is itself internal. If the property needs to be public, the type must also be public, or how would another module know what that type is?

Next you'll create a template for a weather framework that could be used by other apps to access an online weather service via a REST API. This example will help you explore why you set various access levels. Here's the template:

```
public enum Sky {
    case Sunny
    case Cloudy
    //It never rains or snows in our world
}


public struct WeatherDataPoint {
    public var longitude: Float
    public var latitude: Float
```

```
        public var sky: Sky
        public var temp: Float

        public init(longitude: Float, latitude: Float, sky:
➥Sky, temp: Float) {
            self.longitude = longitude
            self.latitude = latitude
            self.sky = sky
            self.temp = temp
        }
    }


public class WeatherService {
    private var simulateCacheHit = true
    public private(set) var dataSourceIdentifier = ""

    public init () { }

    public func getWeatherFor(longitude: Float, latitude:
➥Float) -> WeatherDataPoint? {
        var weatherDataPoint: WeatherDataPoint? =
➥getCachedWeatherFor(longitude, latitude: latitude)
        if let unwrappedWeatherDataPoint = weatherDataPoint {
            return weatherDataPoint
        }

        //we didn't have the data cached, so we request it
        //from the network
        weatherDataPoint = pullWeatherFor(longitude,
➥latitude: latitude)

        if let unwrappedWeatherDataPoint = weatherDataPoint {
            //network pull was successful, cache it for
            //later, for speed and to reduce network access
            //(and costs if you're paying for a weather
            //service)
            cacheWeatherFor(longitude, latitude: latitude,
➥weatherDataPoint: unwrappedWeatherDataPoint)
```

```
        }


        return weatherDataPoint

    }


    private func pullWeatherFor(longitude: Float, latitude:
➥Float) -> WeatherDataPoint? {
        //TODO: pull the data from the API REST service,
        //here we're just always returning a cloudy day
        var pulledWeatherDataPoint: WeatherDataPoint? =
➥WeatherDataPoint(longitude: longitude, latitude:
➥latitude, sky: .Cloudy, temp: 10)
        dataSourceIdentifier = "simulatedPull"
        return pulledWeatherDataPoint
    }


    private func getCachedWeatherFor(longitude: Float,
➥latitude: Float) -> WeatherDataPoint? {
        //TODO: access our disk cache and see if we've
        //already pulled this data point, here we're just
        //always returning a nice sunny day when the cache
        //hits or nil if the cache fails (based on our
        //private simulateCacheHit variable)
        var cachedWeatherDataPoint: WeatherDataPoint? =
➥simulateCacheHit ? WeatherDataPoint(longitude:
➥longitude, latitude: latitude, sky: .Sunny, temp: 30) : nil
        return cachedWeatherDataPoint
    }


    private func cacheWeatherFor(longitude: Float, latitude:
➥Float, weatherDataPoint: WeatherDataPoint) {
        //TODO: save weatherDataPoint to disk
    }
}
```

In this weather framework, you define a `public` enum called `Sky` that stores the general weather description. Then you define a `public struct` `WeatherDataPoint` that contains the details for a place on the planet, and each of the properties are also marked as `public`. One of the properties is `sky` of type `Sky`, using the enumeration just declared ahead of it. Because `WeatherDataPoint` is `public`, and it contains a `public` property of type `Sky`, the `Sky` enumeration must be marked as `public`. If `Sky` were declared with a lower access level, you would get a compile-time error because any code trying to use a `WeatherDataPoint` object wouldn't know how to access the `sky` property.

Next, the main class is `WeatherService`, which is `public`. It has just one `public` method, `getWeatherFor()`, which the app uses to interact with this framework. All the other methods in this class are marked as `private` and are therefore invisible to the rest of the app. The app itself has no idea how the data is pulled, how it's cached, or if there even is a cache, and that's fine. It doesn't matter to the app, and when you mark those functions as `private`, you can be sure no developer is using those methods and possibly messing around with the internal data structures.

If you need to update the framework at some later time, you can safely change any of the `private` or `internal` entities without worrying about breaking another developer's app. You need to be concerned if you're going to make changes to the `public` entities because developers will be using those. So, for instance, if you make changes to `public` entities, such as adding a parameter here or there, all developers using your framework will need to update their code.

In this example, you've also added a `private simulateCacheHit` property to the class. This is for development purposes, so you can test with both cached data and freshly pulled data. The `dataSourceIdentifier` property is a string that identifies which provider you used when you pulled the data. This shows how you've made the property itself `public`, but the `setter` is marked as `private`. `dataSourceIdentifier` is a read-only `public` property.

You just saw that in most situations, the `internal` access level is the default. Notice in the `WeatherService` class that you include a `public init()` closure that does nothing. Because all the properties in this class have default values assigned, the default `init()` closure is sufficient here; you don't need to do any setup or initialization when an instance is created. But the default `init()` closure is `internal` by default. This means that only your module would be able to instantiate a `WeatherService` object. You need to explicitly create an `init()` closure and mark it as `public` so that the app using this framework is able to see and call it.

The same applies to the `WeatherDataPoint` structure: The memberwise initializer that the compiler makes for you to set up the properties is `internal`, and thus the app cannot create its own `WeatherDataPoint` objects; it may only use the ones it receives as return values from the `getWeatherFor()` method. Depending on the API design and intended usage, this may be desirable. For this case, you can see that a developer may need to create her own `WeatherDataPoint` objects, so you've explicitly added a `public init()` method.

There are some special cases in which the default access level will not always be `internal`. In any case where a default access control level of `internal` would expose a type to a higher access level than allowed, the default drops to `private` instead. This can happen, for example, when a method with no explicit access control level uses a `private` type as a parameter. Another case is that if a `class` has a `required init()` method, a subclass that is `public` will have that `required init()` method marked as `public` as well, even if not explicitly indicated.

Exercises

1. Expand on the `NetworkConnection` enumeration to actually detect the current network status. Does it make sense to include this type of functionality in an enumeration? Create a class instead that monitors the network status and uses the `NetworkConnection` enumeration as a property.

2. Create a class that can serve as a general database record, based on the `Record` class you worked with in Section 3.4, "Subclassing." Implement methods to save and retrieve the records from a database. (PLIST or JSON files stored to disk should be sufficient for this exercise.) Implement the subclass `List` that successfully stores items to and retrieves items from the database.

3. Expand on the `Record` and `List` classes you've just created by adding additional overloaded `init()` methods. Can you see that in some instances it's better to overload a method, and in others, adding default values to parameters instead could reduce duplicated code?

4. Look at the `Reversible` protocol and extension from Section 3.11, "Extensions." Because it has only one method, `reverse()`, that mutates the base value, you cannot reverse a constant or literal string. Modify the code so that you can get the reverse value of a constant or literal string as well. Avoid duplicating code by having the `mutating` version of the code use the non-mutating version.

5. Make an extension of `String` that adds subscripting. You should be able to get and set the nth character of the string. How would you handle a subscript that's out of range?

Optionals

Topics in This Chapter

- 4.1 Optionals and `nil`

- 4.2 Validity Checking, Optional Binding, and Forced Unwrapping

- 4.3 Optional Chaining

- 4.4 Implicitly Unwrapped Optionals

- Exercises

In Swift you can use optionals to represent data that can contain an invalid or missing value. In fact, this data structure is used throughout most apps, so it is important to know how to properly use it. When you correctly use optional values, your code is safer to execute because in most cases the compiler will make sure you aren't incorrectly trying to use invalid data in places where you expect something valid. However, using optional values requires you to think differently about how your code works with potentially unknown values. When you begin to use optional types, your code is more descriptive, and you'll have more confidence that you are correctly handling values across your code base.

These are the key points in this chapter:

- Optional types and `nil` in Swift cannot be interchanged with standard value types. This is unlike how "optionals" are represented in Objective-C (`NSNull`, `CGRectNull`, `NSNotFound`).

- Validity checking on optional types checks for the existence of a value and provides a safety check before unwrapping an optional to access its value.

- Optional chaining provides an easy and consistent way to perform multiple operations on optional values without requiring you to individually check and unwrap their values.

- Implicitly unwrapped optionals provide a way to model data that always contains a value after the optional is initialized.

4.1 Optionals and `nil`

Before we dig into how to use optional types in Swift, let's look at some simple examples of how "optional" data is commonly represented in Objective-C so that we will be able to compare it to how similar code works in Swift. One common way to represent invalid or missing data in Objective-C is by using `nil`.

 NOTE

Swift's `nil` represents the absence of valid data of any type and is a literal. On the other hand, in Objective-C, `nil` represents a pointer to an object that doesn't exist. Both languages use the same term, but their meanings are quite different.

Here's an example of creating an `NSString` with the contents of a file:

```
NSString *fileString = [NSString stringWithContentsOfFile:@"somePath"
➥encoding:NSUTF8StringEncoding error:&fileError];
```

If you look at the docs for `+ (instancetype)stringWithContentsOfFile:(NSString *) path encoding:(NSStringEncoding)enc error:(NSError **)error`, you know that you will get `nil` if a file or encoding error is encountered. This seems easy enough to check for in practice, but it requires you, the developer, to do the right thing and handle `nil` appropriately in all situations. When `nil` values aren't explicitly checked, you can run into problems. Here's an overly simple example that illustrates how the behavior of `nil` can lead to unexpected results:

```
NSString *string1 =
  [NSString stringWithContentsOfFile:@"someValidPath"
                              encoding:NSUTF8StringEncoding
                                 error:&fileError];
NSString *string2 =
  [NSString stringWithContentsOfFile:@"invalidPath"
                              encoding:NSUTF8StringEncoding
                                 error:&fileError];
NSString *string3 =
  [NSString stringWithContentsOfFile:@"anotherValidPath"
                              encoding:NSUTF8StringEncoding
                                 error:&fileError];
NSArray *stringArray =

  [NSArray arrayWithObjects:string1, string2, string3, nil];
```

In this example, the value of `string2` would be `nil`, which would terminate the list of objects used to create the array. If later on in the app you assumed that the size of the array were three, you could easily end up with an error by trying to access a value outside the bounds of the array. This could be particularly problematic if the original code used strings that weren't read from a file. Maybe the original implementation didn't need to do bound checks because the values of the strings would never be `nil`. In some situations, an unexpected `nil` can lead to a crash. In this example, you use the same strings read from files, but trying to create an array literal with a `nil` value will produce a crash at runtime:

```
NSArray *stringArray = @[string1, string2, string3];
//Crashes with an NSInvalidArgumentException
```

Now let's look at how the same situation would be handled in a Swift app. You start out with three known strings that are being added to an array:

```
let string1 = "something"
let string2 = "something else"
let string3 = "a third thing"
let stringArray = [string1, string2, string3]
```

Sometime later in development, you change the implementation and read these values from files:

```
let string1 =
  String(contentsOfFile: "someValidPath",
    encoding: NSUTF8StringEncoding, error: &parseError)
let string2 =
  String( contentsOfFile: "invalidPath",
    encoding: NSUTF8StringEncoding, error: &parseError)
let string3 =
  String(contentsOfFile: "anotherValidPath",
    encoding: NSUTF8StringEncoding, error: &parseError)
let stringArray = [string1, string2, string3]
//stringArray: [String?]
```

Here you've used a failable initializer on `String` that returns `String?` (which is shorthand for `Optional<String>`) instead of `String`, and when you make this change, you are going to get a compiler error in every place that those `String` values were used because their type changed. This change in type will require all parts of the code that are affected to be modified in order to handle a potentially nonexistent value.

Using `nil` to represent an invalid value isn't the only way this situation is handled in Objective-C. `NSString` has a property named `integerValue` that will return `0` if the string cannot be parsed into an integer. If you call `indexOfObject:` on an `NSArray` and an index is not found, then the sentinel value of `NSNotFound` is returned. In both of these situations, you run into the same problem that you saw with `nil`. Values of `0` or `NSNotFound` are simply special values of `NSInteger` that you need to handle correctly. In Swift, the type system removes this ambiguity by enforcing the use of `nil` to represent invalid data and by requiring that only optional types can have a value of `nil`.

4.2 Validity Checking, Optional Binding, and Forced Unwrapping

Now you know about the advantages that Swift's optional type gives you, helping you produce safe and readable code when using data that may or may not be present. Now we can talk about how to use optionals in practice. One of the most common ways to use optionals is with `if` statements. Using `if` statements is an easy way to check that an optional contains a value that is expected, and Swift provides some syntactical sugar in the form of data binding to make working with optionals easier. Here's the most basic way to check whether an optional contains a value:

```
if optionalValue != nil {
    //do something
}
```

You cannot use optional types directly in an `if` statement because the generic `enum` optional doesn't implement the `BooleanType` protocol (`enum Optional<T> : Reflectable, NilLiteralConvertible`). The optional value can be either `Some(T)` or `None`, and to check whether the optional contains a value, you verify that the optional is not `nil`. When the optional value is `None`, the optional value is `nil`, and when the value is `Some(T)`, the optional contains a value you can access and use. Let's look at how both of these cases work when doing a basic check for a value. Notice that we unwrap the value of the optional with `!` when you want to use the wrapped value:

```
var optionalSomeValue: String? = .Some("Some")
var optionalNoneValue: String? = .None

if optionalSomeValue != nil {
    println("has a value of \(optionalSomeValue!)")
}
```

```
if optionalNoneValue != nil {

    //won't execute because optionalNoneValue is nil

}
```

In practice, you normally don't need to explicitly specify that an optional is Some(T) or None, and you could rewrite the example like this:

```
var optionalSomeValue: String? = "Some"

var optionalNoneValue: String? = nil
```

This simple example illustrates the importance of thinking about optionals differently than you think about other data types. When an optional is encountered, it can be thought of as an unopened box. The box could contain an object, but it could also be empty. You might know what could be inside the box, but until you actually look inside, you don't know if it is empty or contains what you expect. Continuing with the box analogy, optionals provide a safe way of transporting data across your app, and this is one reason optionals are used frequently in the Swift standard library.

One thing to keep in mind with optionals is that you can safely do an equality check on the value of an optional without first unwrapping the value. The == operator is overloaded and will do the equality check on the value wrapped in the optional, if it exists, and return false if the optional is nil or the equality check fails. What can be misleading about using the == operator is that the check is on the wrapped object and not the optional. The following are a few quick examples that show the use of operators on optionals:

```
let wrappedFalseBool: Bool? = false

if wrappedFalseBool == true {

    //this will not execute

    //the value of the wrapped bool is false

}

if wrappedFalseBool != nil {

    println("True because the optional has a wrapped value")

}


let wrappedInt: Int? = 3

if wrappedInt < 4 {

    println("True because the wrapped value < 4")

}


let nilOptional: Int? = nil

//even though the optional is nil this is a safe operation
```

```
if nilOptional == 3 {
    //won't execute because the optional is nil
}
```

As you saw in Chapter 2, "Diving Deeper into Swift's Syntax," you can use optional binding to make your code less verbose by combining the optional value checking and unwrapping into a single step. You can use optional binding with variables or constants by using the same syntax with either `let` or `var`. You can rework the example above to treat the value in the optional as a variable and modify the object inside the `if` statement. Here's what it looks like:

```
var optionalSomeValue: String? = "Some"
if var foundString = optionalSomeValue {
    foundString += " found value"
    print(foundString)
    //prints "Some found value"
}
print(optionalSomeValue)
//prints "Optional("Some")"
```

Both forced unwrapping using ! and optional binding can also be used in combination with other types of control flow in Swift. Here's how you can use optionals as part of a `switch` statement using both optional binding and forced unwrapping:

```
let optionalInt: Int? = 7
switch optionalInt {
case .None:
    println(".None")
case .Some(let a) where a < 10:
    println("\(a)")
case .Some(10...100):
    println("\(optionalInt!) is between 10 and 100")
default:
    println("\(optionalInt!) is an Int")
}
```

NOTE

Using `.None` or `.Some` isn't always necessary when you're doing pattern matching on a `switch` statement. This example uses them for clarity, but in practice, you will likely leave them out of your pattern matching so that the code is easier to read. You can replace `.None` with `nil` and remove `.Some` from the second case because the type information can be inferred, but the variable `a` would be the optional type and would need to be unwrapped. However, you can't remove `.Some` from the third case because there is no direct conversion between a `Range` and an `Int?`.

4.3 Optional Chaining

When working with complex sets of data, you may often find yourself working with several layers of optional values. If you had to check each optional individually, you'd quickly end up with code that was complicated to read and cumbersome to work with. Optional chaining in Swift allows you to work with a series of optional values in a single step. This creates an easy way to work with properties, methods, and subscripts of a data set that may contain multiple levels of optional values. To illustrate why optional chaining is important, look at how you could create some classes that represent a nested data set:

```
class Outer {
    var inner: Inner?
}


class Inner {
    var innerInner: InnerInner?
}


class InnerInner {
    var innerMostStr: String?
}
```

Now you can create an optional of the outer object type:

```
let outerOptional: Outer?
```

If later on you wanted to check for `innerMostValue String?`, you might use code that looks like this:

```
if let outVal = outerOptional {
    if let inVal = outVal.inner {
```

```
      if let inInVal = inVal.innerInner {
          if let inMostStr = inInVal.innerMostStr {
              println("Ugly code to print \(inMostStr)")
          }
      }
   }
}
```

This code works, and it's safe, but it isn't expressive in the way that Swift code strives to be. This is the problem that optional chaining solves. You can rewrite the preceding code without losing any safety checks by using optional chaining, as follows:

```
if let inMostStr = outerOptional?.inner?.innerInner?.
➥innerMostStr {
    println("This is much nicer \(inMostStr)")
}
```

The syntax of optional chaining is very similar to that of forced unwrapping. However, you use ? instead of ! to gracefully handle any missing values. This allows for concise syntax without sacrificing the safety that using optionals provides.

Optional chaining is able to provide a safe way of performing multiple actions because it treats an entire series of operations as an optional. At each point in the chain, the existence of the optional value is checked, and if it exists, the operations continue. If at any point along the chain a nil value is encountered, then nil is returned for the entire chain. A side effect of treating the entire series as an optional is that if the last operation normally returns a non-optional value, then it will implicitly be wrapped in an optional. Let's look at what this looks like in practice. First, you can change your InnerInner class to have a non-optional property:

```
class InnerInner {
    var innerMostStr:String = ""
}
```

Next, you can use the property innerMostStr directly as a String:

```
var innerInnerValue = InnerInner()
innerInnerValue.innerMostStr = "Inner Most String"
let innerString:String = innerInnerValue.innerMostStr
```

However, if you access that property by using an optional chain, you can see that what is returned is an `Optional<String>`:

```
var outer = Outer()
var innerValue = Inner()
var innerInnerValue = InnerInner()
outer.inner = innerValue
innerValue.innerInner = innerInnerValue
innerInnerValue.innerMostStr = "Inner Most String"
let innerString = outer.inner?.innerInner?.innerMostStr
//Some("Inner Most String")
```

Try removing the `inner` property to see how the behavior of a chain works when a `nil` value is encountered along the way. The entire chain safely handles the `nil` value, and you can continue as if you were accessing any other optional value. (Try changing the behavior from optional chaining to forced unwrapping by changing `?` to `!`, and you'll encounter a run-time error.) So if a property is an optional value, then optional chaining doesn't change the way that property is used, but if the property is not an optional type, then it will be wrapped in an optional when it is used as part of an optional chain.

As you can see, optional chaining provides a convenient way to work with nested optional properties, but you can also use this technique with more than just properties. To see how optional chaining works with methods and subscripting, you need some classes that are more than just a series of single nested properties. The following code defines the classes that will be used to explore optional chaining in more depth:

```
class Student {
    var courses = [SchoolCourse]()

    subscript(i: Int) -> SchoolCourse {
        return courses[i]
    }

    func numberOfCourses() -> Int {
        return courses.count
    }

    func addCourse(c: SchoolCourse) {
        courses.append(c)
    }
```

```
    }

    class SchoolCourse {
        var department: Department?
        let courseName: String

        init(name: String) {
            self.courseName = name
        }

        func printCourseDescription() {
            if let departmentDesc = department?.
➥departmentDescription() {
                println("\(self.courseName) is part of
➥\(departmentDesc)")
            }
            else {
                println(self.courseName)
            }
        }
    }

    class Department {
        var departmentName: String?
        var collegeOf: String?

        func departmentDescription() -> String? {
            if departmentName != nil {
                return departmentName
            }
            else if collegeOf != nil {
                return collegeOf
            }
            else {
                return nil
            }
        }
    }
```

With these classes, we can look at several of the ways to use optional chaining. If you look at the printCourseDescription() function in the SchoolCourse object, you can see an example of calling a function that returns an optional type in an optional chain. This looks exactly like accessing a property because calling a function that returns an optional type behaves the same way as accessing a property. Look what happens if you call a function that returns a non-optional type:

```
let student = Student()
student.addCourse((SchoolCourse(name: "math")))
let optionalStudent: Student? = student
let numOfClasses = optionalStudent?.numberOfCourses()
//Some(1)
```

In this code you create a Student and add a new SchoolCourse to its courses array before wrapping it in an optional. Then you create an optional chain from the Student? and a call to the numberOfCourses() function. What gets returned is the result of numberOfCourses(), but it's wrapped in an optional. Now you know that you can call any function that returns an object, and it will be treated just like a property and return an optional value when called as part of an optional chain.

With very little extra syntax, you can extend optional chaining on any number of functions with return values. If a function returns an optional, then a question mark needs to be added after the parentheses, but if the function returns a non-optional, then the question mark isn't needed. Here's an example:

```
let student = Student()
let mathCourse = SchoolCourse(name: "math")
let mathDepartment = Department()
mathDepartment.departmentName = "Math Department"
mathCourse.department = mathDepartment
student.addCourse(mathCourse)
let optionalStudent: Student? = student
let longChain = optionalStudent?[0].department?.
➥departmentDescription()?.substringToIndex(4).
➥substringFromIndex(1)
```

Let's break down each step of the last line to see how the different pieces of an optional chain fit together. The first piece is optionalStudent?[0], and you put the question mark before the subscript operation because optionalStudent is an optional. You perform the subscript normally because there was a value. The next two pieces, department? and departmentDescription()?, follow the same pattern of adding a question mark before calling the next piece in the chain because both of these operations return optionals. The first substring function isn't followed by a question mark because `substringToIndex` returns a `String`. Finally, the last piece of the function chain is called normally.

4.4 Implicitly Unwrapped Optionals

There are times when your data has the characteristic of always being valid after it is initially set. This doesn't match a non-optional value because before the initial value is defined, the value is `nil`, but it is also a poor fit for an optional because you don't want to have to check for `nil` after it's been set. For this situation, Swift has a special kind of optional called an *implicitly unwrapped optional.*

The main differences between an optional and an implicitly unwrapped optional are how they are defined and how their data is accessed after being created. For other areas, such as optional binding, an implicitly unwrapped optional should be treated the same as a standard optional. To create an implicitly unwrapped optional, you use an exclamation point instead of a question mark:

```
var regularOptional: String? = "Regular"

var implicitlyUnwrapped: String! = "Implicitly unwrapped"
```

 NOTE

Although `ImplicitlyUnwrappedOptional` can be treated the same as a standard `Optional` in most areas, it is its own type of `enum` and not directly related to `Optional`.

The value of an implicitly unwrapped optional is assumed to be set, so when accessing the value, there is no need to use forced unwrapping. Notice that you don't need to use `!` to access the wrapped value:

```
var regularString: String = regularOptional!

var implicitString: String = implicitlyUnwrapped
```

 CAUTION

Implicitly unwrapped optionals require you to make sure that a valid value is assigned before trying to access the value. If you don't assign a value, then you will encounter an error when using an implicitly unwrapped optional in the same way that you will encounter an error if you try to force unwrap an optional that is `nil`.

You most commonly use implicitly unwrapped optionals when you are handling initialization of interdependent objects and when you're interacting with properties of Objective-C classes. As you learned in Chapter 3, "Objects and Classes," classes need to set an initial value for all properties before they can be used, and this can create a unique situation when two objects have an interdependency between each other. Here's an example of this type of relationship:

```
class Mother {
    let name: String
    let firstBorn: FirstBorn!

    init(name: String, firstBornsName: String) {
        self.name = name
        self.firstBorn = FirstBorn(name: firstBornsName, mother:
➡self)
    }
}


class FirstBorn {
    let name: String
    unowned let mother: Mother

    init(name: String, mother: Mother) {
        self.name = name
        self.mother = mother
    }
}
```

In this example, you need to be able to pass the Mother object to the initializer of FirstBorn, but it needs to be fully initialized before you can use it as a parameter. To satisfy the requirement of being fully initialized when self is used in the line self.firstBorn = FirstBorn(name: firstBornsName, mother: self), the property firstBorn is marked as an optional. When you make it an optional, it has the default value of nil, but treating it as a normal optional would require unwrapping the value every time it's used, and you know that it is always going to contain an actual value because it is set in the initializer. By using an implicitly unwrapped optional, you can safely initialize objects with this type of interdependency without creating overly complex code. You should use implicitly unwrapped optionals only when you can guarantee the behavior of always having a value after the initial creation. If there is any chance that the value could change to nil, then you need to use a normal optional.

Exercises

1. Create your own simplified implementation of an optional. This type should be able to represent the cases of `None` and `Some(T)` while also providing ways to check for the existence of and to access wrapped values.

2. Create a function that takes an array of `Strings` and another `String` and returns an `Int?` containing the index of the found string using a case-insensitive search of the array.

3. In what situation would you want to do a direct comparison to an optional's value by using the `==` or `!=` operator? Does this situation take into account all possible values that the optional can contain? In what situation could it be problematic to directly compare an optional's value, and why?

4. Create an array that contains all the files in your app's main bundle. Create a generator for this sequence. Use a `while` loop to iterate over the values returned from the generator's `next()` function to print all the file names.

5. Create your own (simplified) implementation of `ImplicityUnwrappedOptional`. This type should be able to represent the cases of `None` and `Some(T)` and should have a check to see if there is a wrapped value. It should always try to access the wrapped value, which is assumed to exist.

6. Find a group of classes in one of your existing projects (or create new ones) that contains a property that could be represented as an `ImplicityUnwrappedOptional`. What steps do you need to take to make sure all objects are initialized correctly? Is there any possibility that the `ImplicityUnwrappedOptional` is `nil` after initialization? Try making the property a non-optional value and notice the errors that the compiler produces.

For Exercises 7–10, use the following function to get weather data from the web API at http://openweathermap.org/weather-data:

```
func weatherDataForCity(city: String, closure:
➥(json: NSDictionary) -> ()) {
    var urlString = "http://api.openweathermap.org/data/
➥2.5/weather?q=" + city
    var url = NSURL(string: urlString)

    if url == nil {
        return
    }

    let task = NSURLSession.sharedSession().
➥dataTaskWithURL(url!) {(data, response, error) in
        var jsonError: NSError?
```

```
            let json = NSJSONSerialization.JSONObjectWithData(
    ➥data, options: NSJSONReadingOptions.MutableContainers,
    ➥error: &jsonError) as NSDictionary
            closure(json: json)
        }

        task.resume()
    }

    //Sample usage
    weatherDataForCity("Chicago") {(json) in
        println(json)
    }
```

7. Use optional binding to check for and print the ID of the city. Test your result with an invalid city name.

8. Use optional chaining to check for and print the amount of rain that is forecasted for the next three hours.

9. Create a Weather class that represents the returned value from this API. Then modify the weatherDataForCity function to create an object that contains an instance of this newly created class if weather data is available.

10. Modify the weatherDataForCity function to pass NSDictionary? to the closure and gracefully handle errors that can occur in the dataTaskWithURL and JSONObjectWithData steps.

♦ ♦ ♦   **C H A P T E R 5**

Generics

Topics in This Chapter

Generic programming involves defining algorithms in such a way that they are type agnostic, with the actual types involved specified later, when the algorithm is used. By programming using generics, you can create generic templates for functions and/or data types by abstracting the functionality away from specific types. This allows you to focus on writing code but writing code that is powerful and also easy to maintain. Generics, which will be new to Objective-C developers, are an important concept in Swift. Swift uses generic functions and generic types to help reduce duplicate code while still making use of the language's strong type requirements to ensure that variables are always the type you expect. Using generics lets you focus on how you are interacting with your data by defining what kind of data you need and having the compiler create the type-specific code you need. You can make assumptions about data and act on those assumptions without the overhead of having to check whether they're correct since they are guaranteed by the compiler. For example, if you have an array that you expect to contain Ints, you can be sure that it does because the array would be defined to only accept Ints. The same is true for generic types that you define.

These are the key points in this chapter:

- By using generic functions, you can create prototype functions to reduce duplicating code for various types.

- Type parameters let the compiler know what types are valid for your generics.

- You can create generic types to make complex data structures that rely on other simpler types.

- You can extend generic types in a similar manner to how you extend other types.

- By using associated types, you can define protocols that can work with a wider range of types while retaining type safety.

- You can add a `where` clause to the type parameters to enforce more complicated requirements, including restricting the type based on its associated types.

5.1 Why Generics?

Swift is a strongly typed language, which means you must indicate the type of every variable and parameter used. A function that accepts two `Int` values and returns their sum cannot accept two `UInts` and add those together because `Int` and `UInt` are different types. One possible solution to this problem is to overload the function by providing two separate functions with the same name, one taking `Ints`, and another taking `UInts`. Obviously, this will become tedious and is impractical as the number of types the function can work with increases. In just a simple case, you would need to handle the 8-, 16-, 32-, and 64-bit signed and unsigned versions of `Int`—a total of at least 8 functions. In Swift, a more elegant solution is to create generic functions, functions that provide prototype function definitions that the compiler can use to build the multitude of overloaded functions that would be required, automatically, as needed.

5.2 Generic Functions

The syntax of a generic function is similar to that of a normal function declaration, with the addition of a list of type parameters the function is capable of working with.

Here's an example of a generic function that will take any type as its sole parameter:

```
func isASubclassOfNSObject<T>(objectToTest: T) -> Bool {
    return objectToTest is NSObject
}
```

After the function name, you have a parameter list inside angle brackets: `<` `>`. This list tells the compiler which of the types in the rest of the function are placeholders for real types to be supplied later when the function is called. In this case, you use a single type parameter called `T`. The rest of the function indicates that you have one parameter, `objectToTest` of type `T` (the actual type will be determined later), and it returns a Boolean.

The implementation of the function tests whether the supplied parameter is a subclass of `NSObject` and returns `true` if it is and `false` otherwise:

```
println(isASubclassOfNSObject(String()))
//output: true
println(isASubclassOfNSObject(NSString()))
//output: true
println(isASubclassOfNSObject([Int]))
//output: false
println(isASubclassOfNSObject(NSArray()))
//output: true
println(isASubclassOfNSObject([String:Int]))
//output: false
println(isASubclassOfNSObject(NSDictionary()))
//output: true
```

Notice how you declare only a single function, but you are still able to call it with multiple types of values. You can already see how a simple generic function can reduce the amount of code you need to write and maintain.

5.2.1 Type Parameters

The preceding example accepts any object as a parameter, but in practice you'll usually want to restrict which types are acceptable to your function. You handle this by adding constraints to the *type parameters*. As with the syntax you use to indicate that an object will conform to a protocol, you append a colon to the type placeholder and follow with a protocol that the type must conform to:

```
func sumValues<T: IntegerType>(value1:T, value2:T) -> T {
    return value1 + value2
}
```

Here you add a constraint on `T` that it must conform to the protocol `IntegerType`. Any of the 8-, 16-, 32-, or 64-bit versions of `Int`, signed or unsigned, is acceptable and can be handled by the function. `String`s and other non-`Int` types passed to this function will now generate compile-time errors since they do not meet the specified requirements.

5.2.2 Using More Than One Type Parameter

In the previous example, you used only one type parameter, and you called it T. You can use more than one type parameter by listing the parameters, separated by commas. You can also give the types more descriptive names to increase the readability of the code:

```
func existingOrDefaultValue<KeyType:Hashable,
➡ValueType>(dict:[KeyType:ValueType], key:KeyType,
➡defaultValue:ValueType) -> ValueType {
    if let existingValue = dict[key] {
        return existingValue
    }
    return defaultValue
}
```

This generic function gives the type parameters more meaningful names so that future readers of the code have a better idea of what the types are used for.

5.3 Generic Types

Swift gives you the ability to create generic types. A *generic type* is a new data type that relies on one or more other types but is a different type altogether. You're already familiar with two important generic types, Array and Dictionary. As you've seen, both Array and Dictionary depend on having their types defined because they are generic types. An Array of Ints is a completely different type than a single Int, and it's also a different type than an Array of Strings. Dictionaries in Swift are generic types that rely on two types: one for the key (that must conform to the Hashable protocol) and one for the value stored (that doesn't need to conform to any protocol).

Let's look at how to create a generic type to represent a carousel, which is a data structure that keeps items in an endless cycle. Once an item has been added, there's always a next item available since the next item will cycle around to the beginning once it reaches the end. A carousel is useful for creating effects such as an infinite scroll view or an endless cover flow effect.

Here's how you create the generic type to represent the carousel:

```
class Carousel<T> {
    var items = [T]()
    var currentPosition = 0
```

```
    var count: Int {
        return items.count
    }

    var isEmpty: Bool {
        return items.isEmpty
    }

    func append(item: T) {
        items.append(item)
    }

    func next() -> T? {
        if self.isEmpty {
            return nil
        }

        let nextItem = self[currentPosition]
        currentPosition = (currentPosition + 1) % self.count

        return nextItem
    }

    subscript(position: Int) -> T? {
        if self.isEmpty {
            return nil
        }

        return items[position % self.count]
    }
}
```

Now you can make some `Carousel` objects of different types:

```
var intCarousel = Carousel<Int>()
intCarousel.append(1)

var stringCarousel = Carousel<String>()
stringCarousel.append("Hello")
```

NOTE

Notice how when you use the generic type `Carousel`, you need to include the type of data it will contain.

You define a class called `Carousel` that will work with any type `T`. This `T` type doesn't need to be any specific type and doesn't need to conform to any protocols. The `Carousel` class can be used with any type from a simple `Int` to a `UIView` or any other custom type you define. Inside the carousel, you store the items in an array of type `T`, and the array defaults to an empty array. You store the current position in the carousel in a property called `currentPosition`. The `count` computed property is passed through to the `items` array and always returns an `Int`, regardless of the type of `T`.

Another computed property, `isEmpty`, is a shortcut for testing whether the item count is equal to `0`. The `append()` method takes one `item` parameter that must be of type `T` that will be appended to the `items` array. The real heart of this data structure is the `next()` method. It takes no parameters but returns an optional `T`. As long as the carousel has at least one item in it, the optional will contain a value inside; it will be `nil` only if the carousel is empty. When you call `next()`, it moves the `currentPosition` property up by one and then uses the modulus operator `%` to ensure that the value is within your range of items.

A generic type is just like any other type in that it can be extended through extensions and/or made to conform to protocols. Next you'll use an extension to make `Carousel` conform to the `Printable` protocol. Swift defines the `Printable` protocol as:

```
protocol Printable {
    var description: String { get }
}
```

This means you only need to add a `description` computed property and declare that `Carousel` conforms to the protocol:

```
extension Carousel: Printable {
    var description: String {
        return "\(count) items in Carousel"
    }
}
```

This extension declares that `Carousel` will now conform to `Printable`, and it provides the `description` computed property to actually be printed when required. This is as much detail you can give about the `Carousel` object, however. Since you haven't enforced that T conforms to any protocols, you are not able to print any details about the actual items in the carousel because you have no way of knowing what properties or methods may exist on T.

If you alter the definition of Carousel to enforce that T is Printable, you can iterate through items in the description property and use T's description property to construct a more useful description of the carousel:

```
class Carousel<T: Printable> {

    //...

}


extension Carousel: Printable {

    var description: String {

        var description = "Carousel: \n"

        for item in items {

            description += "\t\(item.description)\n"

        }


        return description

    }

}
```

Of course, you can only alter the definition of Carousel because it's a class you've created. You cannot use extensions to add a requirement to the T type. If Carousel were in a third-party framework, for example, and you wanted to change T to conform to a protocol, you would have to subclass Carousel. Here's an example of subclassing a generic type to add a more restrictive type parameter:

```
class PrintableCarousel<T:Printable>: Carousel<T>, Printable {

    var description: String {

        var description = "Carousel: \n"

        for item in items {

            description += "\t\(item.description)\n"

        }


        return description

    }

}
```

You see here that you create a new generic class `PrintableCarousel` that can be used with any type that conforms to `Printable`. `PrintableCarousel` is a subclass of `Carousel<T>`, and it conforms to the `Printable` protocol.

 NOTE

Any subclass of a generic type must also be a generic type.

5.3.1 Associated Types

In Chapter 3, "Objects and Classes," you saw how to define protocols that a class, structure, or enumeration can conform to. The examples in that chapter included adding computed properties and methods that would be exactly the same for any data structure that conformed to the protocol. There are more complex cases where the computed property or method definition would need to change slightly, based on the types involved.

Consider the following `Traversable` protocol:

```
protocol Traversable {
    var count: Int { get }
    var first: Int? { get }
    var last: Int? { get }

    mutating func previous() -> Int?
    mutating func next() -> Int?
    mutating func reset()
}
```

This protocol defines three computed properties that would presumably give an item count and point to the first and last items in a list. It also defines three methods for traversing back and forth through the list or resetting to the beginning again. The problem with this definition is that although it's a protocol, its application is limited because the properties and methods are locked to the `Int` type. It wouldn't make sense for `Carousel<String>` to conform to this protocol because its items are `String`s, and the protocol requires elements of type `Int`.

This is where associated types come in. Consider this example:

```
protocol Traversable {
    typealias Element

    var count: Int { get }
```

```
    var first: Element? { get }
    var last: Element? { get }

    mutating func previous() -> Element?
    mutating func next() -> Element?
    mutating func reset()
}
```

Here you add a `typealias` of `Element` that any type conforming to this protocol must define, and then you use the type of `Element` as the type for the properties and methods instead of using a hard-coded `Int` type. Now you can make a `Carousel<String>` conform to this protocol, and the results from the properties and methods will actually be useful. You can use an extension to make `Carousel` conform to `Traversable`:

```
extension Carousel: Traversable {
    typealias Element = T

    //count is already provided by the Carousel class
    //var count: Int { get }

    var first: T? {
        if self.isEmpty {
            return nil
        }

        return self[0]
    }

    var last: T? {
        if self.isEmpty {
            return nil
        }

        return self[self.count - 1]
    }

    func previous() -> T? {
        if self.isEmpty {
            return nil
```

```
    }

    currentPosition = (currentPosition == 0) ? self.count
- 1 : (currentPosition - 1) % self.count;
        return self[currentPosition]
    }


    //next() is already provided by the Carousel class
    //mutating func next() -> Element?


    func reset() {
        currentPosition = 0
    }
}
```

 NOTE

Often you can drop the `typealias` line because the compiler will be able to infer its type from the property and method definitions.

5.3.2 The `where` Clause

When creating a generic function or type, you sometimes need to enforce more requirements on the types used. In the earlier `Carousel` example, you changed the definition to enforce the requirement that `T` was `Printable`. When using the `Type: Protocol` format in the list of type parameters, the type can conform to only a single protocol. So if you also want to enforce that `T` is `Hashable`, you need to add a `where` clause:

```
class Carousel<T: Printable where T: Hashable> {
    //...
}
```

After the `where` clause, you can add multiple requirements, separated by commas. This is exactly the same as the above:

```
class Carousel<T where T: Printable, T: Hashable> {
    //...
}
```

You can also use a `where` clause to force requirements on associated types:

```
func find<T:Traversable, E:Equatable where T.Element ==
➥E>(elementToFind:E, source:T) -> Int? {
    var mutableSource = source
    var foundAtIndex: Int? = nil

    mutableSource.reset()

    for i in 0 ..< mutableSource.count {
        if let nextItem = mutableSource.next() {
            if nextItem == elementToFind {
                foundAtIndex = i
                break
            }
        }
    }

    return foundAtIndex
}
```

This `find` function uses a type `T` that must be `Traversable` and a type `E` that must be `Equatable`. You use the `where` clause to require that `T`'s associated type `Element` is of type `E` and thus `Equatable`.

Exercises

1. Starting with the `Carousel` class in Section 5.3, "Generic Types," add methods to do the following:

   - Append all items from an array
   - Insert an item at a specific position
   - Check whether an item exists in the carousel
   - Remove an item
   - Peek at the next item without changing the current position index

2. Continue to expand on the `Carousel` class by making it conform to the `Equatable` protocol. *Hint:* You may need to add additional restrictions on `T`.

3. Create a generic type that implements a FIFO (first-in, first-out) queue.

4. Use generics to implement a linked list. (Extra points for a doubly linked list!)

Functions and Closures

Topics in This Chapter

- 6.1 Functions

- 6.2 Closures

- 6.3 Functional Programming Patterns

- Exercises

Functions in Swift provide a flexible way to break your code into small pieces. The parameters and return value of a function give every function a type. Because a function has a type, it can be treated like any other type, and this allows functions to be used as parameters or return values. Functions are an important part of all Swift programs, and the ability to use them as parameters and return values makes functions a powerful data structure in Swift. It is important to understand how to fully take advantage of all the ways you can use functions.

These are the key points in this chapter:

- Functions can require parameters to be passed by name.

- You can assign a default value to a function parameter.

- You can modify function parameters directly through the use of the `inout` keyword.

- Variadic parameters allow functions to take a variable number of parameters.

- Closures allow developers to abstract blocks of functionality, using a flexible and concise syntax.

- Trailing closures have a special optional syntax that makes them easier to work with.

6.1 Functions

A function has three pieces: parameters, the return type, and the name of the function. To create a function, you use the keyword `func` followed by the name of the function, a comma-separated list of parameters inside a set of parentheses, and optionally the return arrow `->` followed by the return type. You write the body of the function inside a set of braces. Here's an example of a simple function that takes an `Int` as a parameter and returns a `String`:

```
func simpleFunction(number: Int) -> String {
    return "This function was passed the parameter \(number)"
}
```

Parameters and return values can take many forms. This chapter introduces the most common ways to create both simple and complex functions in Swift.

6.1.1 Parameters

Functions are a basic building block of a Swift program, and you can define parameters for a function in many different ways. This means you can create functions tailored for many different use cases.

The most common use case is to provide a comma-separated list of parameters in the format *parameterName: type*. Here's an example of a function that takes an `Int` and a `String` as parameters. The values passed to the function are accessed through the parameter names defined in the function declaration.

```
func multipleParams(number: Int, words: String) {
    println("This function was passed \(number) and \(words)")
}


multipleParams(1, "a string")
//prints This function was passed 1 and a string
```

 NOTE

Every function needs to declare a parameter list, and the parameters passed to the function must always be supplied in the same order in which they are defined. To define a function that doesn't have any parameters, you use an empty list `()` when defining and calling the function, as in this example:

```
func noParameterFunction() {
    println("No parameters needed")
}
noParameterFunction()
//prints No parameters needed
```

6.1.2 External Parameter Names

In the previous example, the functions declared had only local parameter names. Local parameter names are needed so that the parameters can be accessed in the body of the function, but the names that are defined in the function declaration aren't needed by the caller. This is the most common way to define parameters because it is usually clear what the purpose of the parameters is. However, sometimes the intention of the function can be clearer to the caller if you require the parameters to be passed by name. You can achieve this by supplying external parameter names to the function declaration. External parameter names are declared before the local parameter name in the list of parameters, like this:

```
func simpleFunction(externalName localName: Int) -> String {
    return "This function was passed the parameter \(localName)"
}
```

When a function is declared with external parameter names, the caller of the function must include these parameter names when calling the function.

Let's look at how to create more readable code by using external parameter names. You can start by creating a function that uses only local parameter names:

```
func update(var a: [String:String], b: String,
➥c: String) -> [String:String] {
    a[b] = c
    return a
}
```

 NOTE

You may have noticed that the first parameter in the previous example begins with the keyword `var`. This is because you are editing the parameter inside the function body and need to mark it as a variable. By default, all parameters are treated as constants and cannot be modified unless they are specified as variables.

When you look at the function definition, you see no indication of what the values of b and c should represent. To use this function correctly, you need to know how the local variables are used because you could easily call the function with the parameters in the wrong order. Here's an example that illustrates the lack of readability of the function previously defined:

```
var dict = ["key":"value"]
var wrongUsage = update(dict, "newValue", "key")
//["newValue": "key", "key": "value"]
var rightUsage = update(dict, "key", "newValue")
//["key": "newValue"]
```

If you change the function to have descriptive external parameter names, it makes the code easier to understand:

```
func update(var a: [String:String], usingKey b: String,
➥withValue c: String) -> [String:String] {
    a[b] = c
    return a
}


var rightUsage = update(dict, usingKey: "key",
➥withValue: "newValue")
```

When calling a function with external parameter names, you must supply the parameters in the correct order, and you must use the external parameter names. By adding semantic meaning to function parameters, you can create code that is much easier to understand in situations that might otherwise be ambiguous.

Sometimes it might make sense for both the local and external parameter names to be the same. To use a local parameter name as an external parameter name, you just need to prefix the parameter name with #. This happens most commonly when you want to add the extra clarity of requiring parameters to be passed by name. Here's what the earlier example looks like when you use this shorthand syntax:

```
func update(var a: [String:String], #key: String,
➥#value: String) -> [String:String] {
    a[key] = value
    return a
}
```

```
var dict = ["key":"value"]
var updated = update(dict, key: "key", value: "newValue")
```

When you define a class function with multiple parameters, by default, the arguments other than the first parameter have an external parameter name that matches the local parameter name, just like this shorthand syntax but without the # prefix. Here's the same update() function, this time declared as a class instance function instead of a global function:

```
class MySwiftClass {

    func update(var a: [String:String], key: String,
➥value: String) -> [String:String] {
        a[key] = value
        return a
    }

    func callClassInstanceFunction() {
        var dict = ["key":"value"]
        var updated = update(dict, key: "key",
➥value: "newValue")
    }

}
```

NOTE

If you want to ignore the external parameter name of a class instance function, you can provide an underscore as the external parameter name so that it is ignored.

6.1.3 Default Parameter Values

Swift makes writing clean and expressive functions easy by allowing you to assign default values to parameters. Default parameter values allow a single function to be called with different sets of parameters, and when a parameter isn't included by the caller, the function uses a predefined value. To define a default value for a parameter, you include = and the value after the type declaration. Here's a simple example:

```
func greet(person: String, withGreeting: String = "Hello") {
    println("\(withGreeting) \(person)")
}
```

If you call this function, you can omit the second parameter, and the function will use the default value, or you can supply all parameters when you call the function:

```
greet("Dave")
//prints "Hello Dave"
greet("Matt", withGreeting: "Hi")
//prints "Hi Matt"
```

 NOTE

Parameters with default values default to having an external parameter name. When only a single parameter name is used in the function declaration, it will be treated as both an external and local parameter name, even though it does not use the shorthand format `#parameterName` and is required when used by the caller.

6.1.4 Variadic and `inout` Parameters

Two types of parameters that are not terribly common but are very useful in some situations are variadic and `inout` parameters. A variadic parameter can take zero or more values as input, and an `inout` parameter allows a function to directly change the value of the parameter.

To make a parameter variadic, you add … after the parameter's type. In the body of the function, the parameter will be represented as an array of the parameters type. Here's an example of a function with a variadic parameter:

```
func max(i: Int, numbers: Int...) -> Int {
    var max = i
    for number in numbers {
        if number > max {
            max = number
        }
    }
    return max
}
```

Now you can call this function with a variable number of parameters (notice that you don't need to include a value for the last parameter):

```
let one = max(1)

let two = max(1, 2)

let three = max(1, 2, 3)

let five = max(1, 2, 3, 4, 5)
```

You could achieve this same behavior by making the last parameter an array, but that would force the caller to manipulate data to match a specific pattern and would result in less readable code. Variadic parameters provide a simple and clean way to write a single function that can be called in a way that is natural to the caller for a variable number of parameters.

 NOTE

A function can contain only one variadic parameter, and it must always be the final argument to the function.

You should generally avoid directly modifying a parameter passed to a function unless it is clear that changes to the parameter are the intended behavior. When this functionality is needed, Swift allows a parameter to be marked as an `inout` parameter, and changes made to the parameter in the body of the function are applied directly to the value that was passed by the caller. To add this behavior to a parameter, you add the keyword `inout` before the parameter name. The caller must also explicitly mark `inout` parameters by prefixing such a parameter with `&` to prevent accidental modification of values. Here's an example of a place that `inout` parameters are used in the standard library:

```
var numbers = [7, 9, 4, 3, 2]


//func sort<T : Comparable>(inout array: [T])
sort(&numbers)


println(numbers)
//prints: [2, 3, 4, 7, 9]
```

The `sort()` function modifies the array that is passed to it, so the caller marks the parameter as `inout`, using the `&` prefix when calling the `sort()` function. You should use `inout` only when the behavior is appropriate and not to mimic having multiple return values. If you need multiple return values, you should use a tuple return type, as described in Chapter 2, "Diving Deeper into Swift's Syntax."

NOTE

By default, the `sort` function sorts using the less-than comparator. If you want to sort using a different predicate, you can supply your own comparator closure. Here's how you would do a greater-than sort:

```
sort(&numbers) { (lhs, rhs) in
  return lhs > rhs
}
```

6.1.5 Return Types

Swift allows you to write functions that are very flexible with what they return. The simplest function doesn't return a value, and the function declaration doesn't even need to specify anything when there is nothing returned:

```
func nothingToReturn() {
    println("No need to write ->")
}
```

 NOTE

Even though you don't need to specify a return value when you declare a function, it will be given a return type of `()`. The complete type of a function with no parameters and no return value is `() -> ()`.

To add a return type to a function, you use a right-arrow `->` followed by the type of the return value. Swift is very powerful because functions can return any type, which means you can create functions that return functions or a tuple (to return multiple values). Let's look at some examples of returning more complicated types from a function. This example might not look too exciting at first glance, but it is an example of the powerful Swift feature of being able to return functions from functions:

```
func customSort() -> (Int, Int) -> Bool {
    func customSortFunc(lhs: Int, rhs: Int) -> Bool {
        return abs(lhs) < abs(rhs)
    }
    return customSortFunc
}
```

```
var numbers = [7, -9, 4, -3, 2]
sort(&numbers, customSort())
println(numbers)
//prints: [2, -3, 4, 7, -9]
```

We'll explore the power behind this feature in Section 6.3, "Functional Programming Patterns," but for now let's focus on understanding what's happening and how that is expressed in the syntax. The `customSort()` function specifies a return type of `(Int, Int) -> Bool`, which means the type of the return value is a function that takes two parameters of type `Int` and returns a `Bool`. All the pieces that follow the first `->` specify the one specific type that the function returns, and the return value can be used anywhere that type is used. In the previous example the `sort` function is declared as:

```
func sort<T>(inout array: [T], predicate: (T, T) -> Bool)
```

You can see that the comparator function created in `customSort()` is the same type as the predicate parameter needed when calling the `sort()` function.

Another powerful type to return from a function is a tuple. Using a tuple type as a return value allows functions to return multiple values in a lightweight and flexible way. Let's say you want to do some processing on an array, and you want to calculate several values. By using a tuple as a return type, you can process the array one time and return all the values in one step. Here's a simple example:

```
func processNumbers(array: [Int]) -> (sum: Int, max: Int) {
    var sum = 0
    var max = Int.min
    for i in array {
        sum += i
        if i > max {
            max = i
        }
    }
    return (sum, max)
}

var numbers = [7, -9, 4, -3, 2]
var results = processNumbers(numbers)
println("Sum = \(results.sum), Max = \(results.max)")
//prints: Sum = 1, Max = 7
```

Notice that you can add semantic value to the tuple in the function declaration, and when you use the result, you have easy-to-read code. This makes returning tuples an ideal use case when you have small pieces of structured data that don't need to be represented by a class.

6.2 Closures

Closures in Swift provide a simple way to isolate pieces of code, using clean and flexible syntax. The ability to write a chunk of code that can take parameters and return values without the overhead of naming and declaring a function makes closures especially useful when functions have function types as arguments or return values. Swift also provides several pieces of syntactical sugar to make working with closures easier. Here's how you could rewrite the `customSort()` example from earlier in this chapter using closure expression syntax:

```
var numbers = [7, -9, 4, -3, 2]
sort(&numbers, { (lhs: Int, rhs: Int) -> Bool in
    return abs(lhs) < abs(rhs)
})
println(numbers)
//prints: [2, -3, 4, 7, -9]
```

 NOTE

The syntax of a closure expression, as introduced in Chapter 2, is the following:

```
{ (parameters) -> return type in
    statements
}
```

Notice how much easier the code is to read for this simple example when you can write the sorting predicate directly in the function call. In cases where you can shortly express the intended purpose, closures will produce much cleaner code than supplying functions as parameters. You can use a closure as a parameter in this case because the closure has the same type as the `customSort()` function from the earlier example (`(Int, Int) -> Bool`). Here's how you could make the example reusable by creating a function that returns a new sorted array:

```
func absSort(arr: [Int]) -> [Int] {
    return arr.sorted { (lhs: Int, rhs: Int) -> Bool in
        return abs(lhs) < abs(rhs)
    }
}
```

```
var numbers = [7, -9, 4, -3, 2]
let absSortedNumbers = absSort(numbers)
println(absSortedNumbers)
//prints: [2, -3, 4, 7, -9]
```

6.2.1 Inferring Parameters and the Return Value

Because the type information of the parameters and the return value is defined in the function declaration, that information can be inferred in the closure. You can rewrite your closure from the preceding section to be more compact by omitting the type information that can be inferred:

```
sort(&numbers, {lhs, rhs in return abs(lhs) < abs(rhs)})
```

One common pattern is for a closure to return a value, and when the closure consists of only a single expression that returns a value, the return keyword can be inferred. Here's what your predicate becomes if you let the return be inferred:

```
sort(&numbers, {lhs, rhs in abs(lhs) < abs(rhs)})
```

These variations allow code to be written in a way that focuses on what is most important to communicate. The behavior of the `sort` function's predicate is obvious, and there isn't any clarity lost by removing the types and return keyword, but in other situations, removing these pieces of information can result in harder-to-read code. It's important to always strive to produce code that focuses on what's important, and sometimes it is best to retain information even when it could be inferred by the compiler.

 NOTE

Closure parameters are automatically given argument names that follow the pattern $0, $1, $2. You can use these default parameters instead of supplying a list of named parameters and the in keyword. Here's what the example from before would look like using this shorthand syntax:

```
sort(&numbers, {abs($0) < abs($1)})
```

You should generally avoid this syntax because of the lack of readability it produces in most cases.

6.2.2 Trailing Closures

Writing a function that takes a function type as the last parameter is a very powerful way to work with your code and is a pattern that you'll notice is used frequently in the Swift standard library. Because this pattern is very useful and is also used so frequently, the Swift compiler provides a cleaner way of working with this situation: *trailing closures*. Trailing closures come after and outside the standard list of parameters. As you can see here, the format of trailing closures closely resembles the format of standard functions:

```
functionBeingCalled(parameter1, parameter2) {
    //Closure expression
}
```

Here's what the `sort` function becomes when you use a trailing closure:

```
sort(&numbers) { lhs, rhs in
    abs(lhs) < abs(rhs)
}
```

Notice that the trailing closure stands out from the rest of the parameters and makes it easier to focus on the behavior of the closure. Let's look at another function in the Swift standard library where trailing closures can be used. The `Array` type provides a `map()` function where a closure can be used to modify the values of the array to produce a new array:

```
var integers = [1, 2, 3, 4, 5]

var mappedValues = integers.map { number in
    number * number
}
println(mappedValues)
//prints: [1, 4, 9, 16, 25]
```

 NOTE

Notice that you call the `map` function without parentheses so that the intended functionality is easier to read. Parentheses are optional for a function that has a closure as the only argument and should usually be left out to reduce the visual clutter of the code.

6.3 Functional Programming Patterns

The topic of functional programming is far beyond the scope of this book, but it is a tool that Swift programmers can take advantage of and is worth a brief look. For now we will explore only the functional programming pattern of building a solution out of several distinct steps that can be combined in a consistent way.

Instead of diving deeply into theory, let's just look at an example. The standard library contains a `reduce()` function that takes a sequence, an initial value, and a transformation function as parameters. You can use this to make several useful pieces of code. Here's what a `sum()` function looks like using `reduce()`:

```
func sum(numbers: [Int]) -> Int {
    return reduce(numbers, 0) { sum, number in
        sum + number
    }
}
```

In this function, you start with an initial value of `0`, and for each element in the array, you add it to the current sum.

Now that you've seen how to write a long-winded `sum()` function, you can modify your code to be more concise. You can call `reduce()` on the array instead of calling the generic `reduce()` function, and you can eliminate a lot of the unnecessary code in the closure:

```
func sum(numbers: [Int]) -> Int {
    return numbers.reduce(0, +)
}
```

You can use the `+` operator function directly because it matches the type required for the `reduce()` function:

```
func +(lhs: Int, rhs: Int) -> Int
```

By combining the operator function and `reduce()` function, you create a new function that has very clear and concise behavior. You can use the same pattern to create a `product()` function:

```
func product(numbers: [Int]) -> Int {
    return numbers.reduce(1, *)
}
```

Now that you've glimpsed the power of composing functions together into more powerful functions, you're ready to see what it's like to write your own functions that can take advantage of this behavior. In the following examples you will write your own more generic version of `reduce()` and a similar function that does the processing in reverse order.

Those who are somewhat familiar with functional programming might recognize that these are implementations of *left fold* and *right fold* higher-order functions. The reason you want two different functions is that not all functions are associative with respect to the order in which elements are processed. If you have a list of `Ints`, the + operator is associative, but the / operator isn't. With parentheses to show the order of processing, you can see that `((1+2)+3)` is equal to `(1+(2+3))`, but `((1/2)/3)` does not equal `(1/(2/3))`. Let's see what these fold functions look like:

```
func foldLeft<T, U>(array: [T], initialValue: U,
➥closure: (U, T) -> U) -> U {
    var foldedValue = initialValue
    for e in array {
        foldedValue = closure(foldedValue, e)
    }
    return foldedValue
}


func foldRight<T, U>(array: [T], initialValue: U,
➥closure: (T, U) -> U) -> U {
    var foldedValue = initialValue
    let reversed = array.reverse()
    for e in reversed {
        foldedValue = closure(e, foldedValue)
    }
    return foldedValue
}
```

Notice that unlike with `reduce()`, which operates on a single type, these functions operate on potentially different types.

Now that you have these functions, let's look at what you can do with them. You can use them in the same way you use `reduce()`, by supplying an operator function:

```
var doubles = [1.0, 2.0, 3.0]

println(foldLeft(doubles, 0.0, +))
//print: 6.0
println(foldRight(doubles, 0.0, +))
//print: 6.0

println(foldLeft(doubles, 1.0, /))
//print: 0.166666666666667
println(foldRight(doubles, 1.0, /))
//print: 1.5
```

Or you can supply a custom closure. Here's an example that uses a custom closure to count the length of an array and uses the result to calculate an average:

```
func average(array: [Double]) -> Double {
    return foldLeft(array, 0.0, +) / foldLeft(array,
➥0.0) { sum, _ in sum + 1}
}
```

```
println(average(doubles))
//prints: 2.0
```

 NOTE

You don't need the values of the array when you are calculating the length in the closure, so you use _ to ignore the parameter values in the closure instead of assigning them to a variable.

Breaking up a problem into a series of smaller pieces that can be represented as functions can help you create powerful programs that are easier to work with and less prone to errors because they operate in a consistent manner. Swift allows you to take advantage of the functional programming paradigm in many ways and is a topic that is worth exploring.

Exercises

For Exercises 1 and 2, use the following class as a starting point:

```
class Person {
    var firstName: String!
    var middleName: String?
    var lastName: String?
    var job: String?
    var age: Int?

    init(firstName: String) {
        self.firstName = firstName
    }
}
```

1. Create a factory function that takes two `String` parameters (`firstName` and `job`) and returns a new `Person` with the correct properties set. Write this function using external parameter names.

2. Rewrite the factory function from Exercise 1 so that the `job` parameter has a default value.

3. Write a function that takes a variable number of `String` parameters and returns an array that contains all the supplied parameters.

4. Write a function that takes two parameters and swaps their values. This function should not return any values.

5. Write a function that takes a variable number of predicates and returns a function that is a combined predicate of the supplied parameters.

6. Write a function that takes an array and a predicate closure and returns an array that contains only the values of the original `Array` parameter that fulfill the predicate closure.

7. Use the `map()` function on `Array` to resample the values of an array of doubles by dividing by the array's average value.

8. Use the `foldLeft()` function introduced in this chapter to write a function that takes an array and returns an array with the elements in reverse order.

9. Use the `foldLeft()` function introduced in this chapter to write a function that takes an array and returns an array that contains no duplicate values.

Working with Objective-C

Topics in This Chapter

- 7.1 Interacting with C and Objective-C APIs

- 7.2 Working with Swift and Objective-C in a Single Project

- Exercises

To create a great app using Swift, you need to work with the Cocoa frameworks and Objective-C classes. Thankfully, Swift was designed for easy compatibility with both Objective-C and all the existing Apple frameworks you'll want to use when creating apps. In this chapter, you'll learn the basics of how to work with existing Cocoa frameworks and Objective-C code in Swift and also how to integrate your new Swift code into an Objective-C project.

These are the key points in this chapter:

- Swift can import Cocoa frameworks and Objective-C classes.

- Some common Objective-C classes are automatically converted to equivalent Swift classes when imported.

- Some Swift types are bridged with their Objective-C counterparts.

- Swift provides specific types for working with C APIs.

- Most Swift code can be imported into and used in Objective-C.

- You can use Swift and Objective-C in the same project.

7.1 Interacting with C and Objective-C APIs

The first step in working with an Apple framework is to import the module into your Swift code. After you import the framework you want to work with, you will have access to all the classes and functions that the framework provides, and certain core classes will be mapped to their Swift-equivalent classes automatically. To import an Objective-C framework, you just need the keyword `import` followed by the name of the framework. Here's an example of importing the Cocoa framework:

```
import Cocoa
```

Once a framework is imported, you can create Swift objects of classes defined in the imported framework. When an Objective-C class is imported into Swift, several conversions happen automatically, and the syntax to initialize an Objective-C class is modified so that it matches Swift conventions. Instead of calling `alloc` and `init`, you initialize classes just as you would a normal Swift class, but the naming of the initializers is changed when the class is imported into Swift. The `init` or `initWith` prefix of the initializer is removed, and only the initializer's arguments are left. The following examples of creating Objective-C classes in Objective-C and Swift illustrate the automatic renaming:

```
//Objective-C:
UIView *view = [[UIView alloc] init];
UIView *viewWithFrame = [[UIView alloc]
➡initWithFrame:CGRectZero];


//Swift:
let view = UIView()
let viewWithFrame = UIView(frame: CGRectZero)
```

> **NOTE**
>
> You may have noticed that the `alloc` method is completely absent from the Swift code above. Swift handles the memory allocation for you, even when you're working with Objective-C types. This means your Swift code also won't have a `dealloc` method for doing cleanup, and you might need to implement a `deinit` function to make sure your classes gracefully end their life cycles.

Once you have objects that are initialized, you can use them in nearly the same way as any other Swift object. You can read and write properties, just as you can in Objective-C:

```
//Objective-C:
view.backgroundColor = [UIColor colorWithWhite:0.5 alpha:0.5];
UIColor *backgroundColor = view.backgroundColor;


//Swift:
view.backgroundColor = UIColor(white: 0.5, alpha: 1.0)
var backgroundColor = view.backgroundColor
```

Because `backgroundColor` is a property, you don't need to add `()` to access the property, as you need to do when calling a function that doesn't take any parameters. Also notice that the factory method in Objective-C was converted to the same syntax used for initializers, so creating objects has a consistent style.

Once you have a value, you can call functions on the object in the same way you would call any other Swift function:

```
//Objective-C:
CGRect frame = CGRectInset(viewWithFrame.frame, 5.0, 5.0);
UIView *subview = [[UIView alloc] initWithFrame:frame];
[viewWithFrame addSubview:subview];


//Swift:
let frame = CGRectInset(viewWithFrame.frame, 5.0, 5.0)
var subview = UIView(frame: frame)
viewWithFrame.addSubview(subview)
```

Objective-C types with functions that take multiple arguments look almost the same as they do in Objective-C when they are called in Swift. The first parameter is passed without an external name, but the rest of the parameters are passed using an external name. Here's an example:

```
//Objective-C:
CGRect frame = CGRectInset(viewWithFrame.frame, 5.0, 5.0);
UIView *anotherView = [[UIView alloc] initWithFrame:frame];
[viewWithFrame insertSubview:anotherView aboveSubview:subview];


//Swift:
let frame = CGRectInset(viewWithFrame.frame, 5.0, 5.0)
var anotherView = UIView(frame: frame)
viewWithFrame.insertSubview(anotherView, aboveSubview:subview)
```

7.1.1 Optional Properties and Return Values

In most cases, classes that are imported from Objective-C behave like normal Swift classes, but two situations to pay close attention to are functions that return optionals (including `init` methods that may fail and return `nil`) and functions that return objects of type `AnyObject`. Objective-C doesn't have an optional type, so functions that would return `nil` in Objective-C have been modified to return an optional when called from Swift, and these situations require slightly different handling in Swift. Let's look at `UIView`'s method `viewWithTag` to see an example of this behavior and how to properly handle it in Swift. If you write code that doesn't check for a valid returned object, you will end up with code that either doesn't compile or that crashes at run time.

```
//Objective-C:
//This code doesn't produce a crash at run time
//sending messages to nil is OK in Objective-C
UIView *viewDoesntExist = [viewWithFrame viewWithTag:1];
[viewDoesntExist addSubview:anotherView];


//Swift:
//This code will compile, but it will
//crash when viewWithTag returns nil
//func viewWithTag(tag: Int) -> UIView?
let viewDoesntExist = viewWithFrame.viewWithTag(1)
//forced unwrapping the value returned from
//an Objective-C framework isn't safe
viewDoesntExist!.addSubview(anotherView)
```

To create safe code when interacting with classes that return optionals, you need to check the return values in the same way you normally handle regular optionals:

```
var viewMightExist = viewWithFrame.viewWithTag(1)
if let viewDoesExist = viewMightExist {
    viewDoesExist.addSubview(anotherview)
}
```

You will commonly see optionals used as properties of an Objective-C based class. Let's take a look at some of the properties for `UIImageView`:

```
var image: UIImage? // default is nil
var highlightedImage: UIImage? // default is nil
```

Both of these properties might not be present at run time, and so it is important to check for a valid value when you access properties that are optionals. You can use data binding to create a variable and check for the existence of the value in a single step:

```
var imageView = UIImageView(frame: CGRectZero)
//...
if let image = imageView.image {
    //here we can safely use the image property
}
```

7.1.2 `AnyObject` Types

When using Objective-C frameworks in Swift, you often need to work with `AnyObject` types. In Objective-C, it is common for a function to return a value of type `id` when the value that is returned can take many forms; when it is imported into Swift, the `id` type is converted to the `AnyObject` type. When you encounter an `AnyObject` type value, it is important that you handle the object in a safe way to avoid run-time crashes.

One function that returns an `AnyObject?` type is `NSJSONSerialization.JSONObjectWithData()`. To safely use the return value of this function, you need to make sure that it contains a valid value and also that you convert the value to the correct type for use in code later. If you expect the return value to be a specific type, then you can use optional chaining and type casting. Here's an example of handling an expected return value of an `NSDictionary`:

```
var jsonResult: AnyObject? = NSJSONSerialization.
➥JSONObjectWithData(data, options: nil, error: nil)

if let jsonDict = jsonResult as? NSDictionary {
    //We now have a valid NSDictionary
}
```

For other situations, you might want to handle several different return types, and you can use a `switch` statement to safely check for different results. First, you check to see if you have a valid `AnyObject`, and then you use pattern matching to find the return type:

```
var jsonError: NSError?
let jsonOptional: AnyObject! = NSJSONSerialization.
➥JSONObjectWithData(data, options: nil, error: &jsonError)
if let json: AnyObject = jsonOptional {
```

```
    switch json {
    case let jsonDict as NSDictionary:
        println(jsonDict)
    case let jsonArray as NSArray:
        println(jsonArray)
    default:
        println("Unknown \(json)")
    }
}
else {
    //handle this potential error
}
```

7.1.3 Subclassing, Extensions, and Protocols

Now that you know how to work with Objective-C classes that have been imported into Swift, let's explore how to extend those classes to fit your needs through the use of subclassing, extensions, and protocols.

To subclass an Objective-C class, all you need to do is follow the same syntax as for subclassing a Swift class. Here's an example:

```
class MySwiftViewController: UIViewController {


}
```

If your subclass needs to implement protocols, then you simply add them as a comma-separated list after the superclass:

```
class MySwiftViewController: UIViewController,
➥UITableViewDataSource, UITableViewDelegate {

    func tableView(tableView: UITableView,
➥numberOfRowsInSection section: Int) -> Int {
        return 0
    }

    func tableView(tableView: UITableView,
➥cellForRowAtIndexPath indexPath: NSIndexPath) ->
➥UITableViewCell {
```

```
        return UITableViewCell(frame: CGRectZero)
    }
}
```

When you subclass an Objective-C class, you need to follow the Swift conventions and rules for initialization. If you need to add behavior that would be handled in `dealloc` in Objective-C, you can add a deinitializer: `deinit`. Here's what a subclass might look like with a custom initializer and deinitializer:

```
class ViewController: UIViewController {

    var specialString: String!

    deinit {
        NSNotificationCenter.defaultCenter().
➥removeObserver(self)
    }

    init(specialString: String) {
        self.specialString = specialString
        super.init(nibName: nil, bundle: nil)

        NSNotificationCenter.defaultCenter().addObserver(
            self,
            selector: "handleNotification:",
            name: "SpecialNotification",
            object: nil
        )
    }

    required init(coder aDecoder: NSCoder) {
        super.init(coder: aDecoder)
    }

    func handleNotification(sender: AnyObject) {
        println("got the special notification")
    }
}
```

7.1.4 Automatically Converted Types

Several major classes are automatically converted between Swift and Objective-C types to make interoperability easier. These data types are known as *bridged types*, and the Swift and Objective-C types can be freely interchanged so that most of the time you don't need to convert or cast values to a different type. For example, any functions that take `NSString` parameters can be passed a Swift `String`, and functions that normally return an `NSString` value are automatically converted to return a `String`. Let's look at some examples of how `String` values get automatically bridged to `NSString` values.

If you want to set the text of a `UILabel` in Objective-C, you use an `NSString`, but in Swift you can pass a `String` without running into a type conflict:

```
//Objective-C
UITextField *textField = [[UITextField alloc] init];
textField.text = @"Obj-C NSString";


//Swift
var textField = UITextField()
textField.text = "Swift String"
```

Another advantage of being able to seamlessly convert between `String` and `NSString` is that you can use all the functionality of `NSString` that isn't available in `String`. After importing the Foundation framework, you can use any function in `NSString` as if it were a part of `String`. Here's an example of calling a function that's part of `NSString` but isn't available as part of Swift's `String` class:

```
var string1 = "NSString and String"
var string2 = "nsarray and array"
var prefix = string1.commonPrefixWithString(string2,
➥options: .CaseInsensitiveSearch)
//"NS"
```

NOTE

Because `String` and `NSString` are bridged, you can cast between the two types using the `as` keyword, without having to worry about the cast failing, but you will rarely need to explicitly use a specific type due to the way the default behavior of importing Objective-C code into Swift converts `NSString` usages to `String`.

For numbers, you can automatically bridge to `NSNumber` from `Int`, `UInt`, `Float`, `Double`, and `Bool`. However, you can't use `NSNumber` when a Swift number type is required because of the way that an `NSNumber` can contain several kinds of values. When you have an `NSNumber`, you can cast it to the Swift number type that is needed. Here's an example of the seamless conversion to `NSNumber` and a safe conversion back to a Swift type:

```
var swiftDouble = 3.14

var nsnumberDouble: NSNumber = swiftDouble

var backToSwift = nsnumberDouble as Double
```

Working with the Objective-C collections `NSArray` and `NSDictionary` is similar to working with `NSNumber`. You can use Swift's `Array` or `Dictionary` in places that expect `NSArray` or `NSDictionary`, but converting to Swift requires a little bit of extra work. When you convert an `NSArray` to an `Array`, you get an `[AnyObject]` because an `NSArray` can contain any Objective-C classes; without checking the actual values of the array, you can only know that the values subclass `AnyObject`. If you want to have an array of a more specific type, then you need to try to downcast the `[AnyObject]` to the desired type and check whether the downcast was successful. Here's what this looks like:

```
let numbers = [1, 2, 3]

let nsarray: NSArray = numbers

let backToSwift: [AnyObject] = nsarray

if let downcastArray = backToSwift as? [Int] {
    println("Safely back to Swift")
}
```

`NSDictionary` has the same behavior as `NSArray`, and converting an `NSDictionary` to Swift will result in an `[AnyObject: AnyObject]`. You can use the same technique of downcasting to see if the values contained in the `NSDictionary` meet a specified type requirement. Here's what working with `NSDictionary` might look like:

```
let swiftDict = [1:"one", 2:"two"]

let nsdict: NSDictionary = swiftDict

if let backToSwift = nsdict as? [Int:String] {
    println("Safely back to Swift")
}
```

The technique of using `as?` to safely check whether a value can be downcast to a specific type can help you check whether an object is a kind of type or conforms to a protocol. Two situations where this might be used are when a target is given an `AnyObject` type from a user interaction event and when checking whether a delegate conforms to a given protocol. Here's what both of these examples might look like:

```
@IBAction func touchUpInside(sender: AnyObject) {
    if let button = sender as? UIButton {
        //Do something with the UIButton
    }
}


if let tableViewDelegate = delegate as? UITableViewDelegate {
    //work with the delegate
}
```

7.1.5 Selectors and Enums

When you're working with Objective-C classes, there are times when you need to work directly with selectors. Swift makes working with selectors easy by representing an Objective-C selector as a Swift structure of type `Selector` and by allowing you to automatically convert a `String` to a `Selector`. Here's how you can add an action selector to an Objective-C class in Swift. First, you create a normal function that will be the action:

```
func touchCancel(sender: AnyObject) {
    println("Touch cancel")
}
```

Next, you can add the target action. Notice that the string literal is automatically converted to the `Selector` type and that a colon is added so that the selector syntax matches what is expected for Objective-C selector naming:

```
if let button = UIButton.buttonWithType(.DetailDisclosure)
➥as? UIButton {
    button.addTarget(self,
        action: "touchCancel:",
        forControlEvents: .TouchCancel)
}
```

In this example you were able to use Swift-style enumeration `.DetailDisclosure` to specify the type of button because the Objective-C enumeration for `UIButtonType` was declared with the `NS_ENUM` macro. When a C-style enum is written with the `NS_ENUM` macro, Swift is able to import the enumeration as a Swift enumeration and can take advantage of all the features of Swift enumerations. Here's what the `UIButtonType` enumeration looks like in Objective-C and Swift to show the advantage of using the `NS_ENUM` macro:

```
//Objective-C:
typedef NS_ENUM(NSInteger, UIButtonType) {
    UIButtonTypeCustom = 0,
    UIButtonTypeSystem NS_ENUM_AVAILABLE_IOS(7_0),

    UIButtonTypeDetailDisclosure,
    UIButtonTypeInfoLight,
    UIButtonTypeInfoDark,
    UIButtonTypeContactAdd,

    UIButtonTypeRoundedRect = UIButtonTypeSystem,
};


//Swift:
enum UIButtonType : Int {
    case Custom // no button type
    case System // standard system button

    case DetailDisclosure
    case InfoLight
    case InfoDark
    case ContactAdd
}
```

7.1.6 Working with C Code

There are times when you might need to interact directly with C code, and Swift provides several useful types for this situation. For working directly with primitive data types, Swift provides C-style types that map directly to specific C primitive types. These types follow the pattern of the capital letter C followed by a *camel-cased name* for the primitive type. For example, `bool` becomes `CBool`, and `unsigned long long` becomes `CUnsignedLongLong`. This same naming pattern is also used for pointer types, but pointer types in Swift have some added semantic value. For example, the C pointer type `const void *` becomes `CConstVoidPointer` in Swift, and `void *` becomes either `CMutableVoidPointer` or `COpaquePointer`, depending on whether the value is a parameter or a return value. For a pointer that expects a specific type, you use the same syntax you would use for other generic types and put the specific type to use inside a set of < >. For example, a mutable pointer to a specific type has the syntax CMutablePointer<Type>, which would look like CMutablePointer<Int> if the pointer was for the type Int. Here's an example of a function that takes some colors and returns a gradient by using the C-based Core Graphics framework:

```
func createGradientWithColors(colorSpace:CGColorSpace,
➥startColor:CGColor, endColor:CGColor) -> CGGradient {
    let locations: [CGFloat] = [0.0, 1.0]
    let colors: CFArray = [startColor, endColor]
    //func CGGradientCreateWithColors(space: CGColorSpace!,
➥colors: CFArray!, locations: ConstUnsafePointer<CGFloat>)
➥-> CGGradient!
    let gradient = CGGradientCreateWithColors(colorSpace,
➥colors, locations)
    return gradient
}
```

Notice how the locations array is declared with the type [CGFloat] and then is used for the parameter that takes ConstUnsafePointer<CGFloat>. This works because in C, it's valid to pass a typed array as a pointer argument. In Swift, a function that takes a C pointer type as a parameter can accept any type that would be considered valid based on the underlying C behavior.

Swift was designed to easily integrate with Cocoa and Objective-C projects, while still maintaining the additional type safety that Swift provides. In some cases, you need to use a slightly different pattern in Swift, and using code from an Objective-C project requires a little more attention to make sure you handle objects correctly. But in most situations, integrating Objective-C code into your Swift projects is an easy task.

7.2 Working with Swift and Objective-C in a Single Project

Now that you've seen how to work with Objective-C frameworks in Swift, it's time to see how we can work with Swift and Objective-C files in a single project. Because Swift was designed to be highly compatible with Objective-C, it's easy to use your own Objective-C classes in Swift, and you can also expose functionality written in Swift to Objective-C classes.

Any Objective-C files that are in a project that you want to expose to Swift code in the same project need to be included in the Objective-C bridging header file. In this bridging header file, you include import statements for all the Objective-C header files with code that you want to access from Swift. All the code that is publicly exposed in the header files imported in the bridge header file will automatically be available in any Swift code files in the project. Once you have the bridging header set up you have access to all the functionality of your Objective-C classes:

```
//Project-Bridging-Header.h

//contains #import "MyAwesomeObjCClass.h"

var object = MyAwesomeObjCClass()

object.awesomeObjCFunction()
```

 NOTE

The first time you add a Swift file to an existing Objective-C project, Xcode prompts you to make the bridge header file.

Xcode also makes it easy to use Swift code within Objective-C classes by automatically generating the necessary headers to expose Swift classes for use in Objective-C. To import a Swift class into an Objective-C file, you simply use a normal import statement, like this:

```
#import "ProductModuleName-Swift.h"
```

Because this header is generated by Xcode, it follows the same format of the name of the module that contains the Swift code followed by a -Swift.h postfix. This single file will import all the publicly exposed Swift code.

When you import Swift code into Objective-C, you need to treat that code like a normal Objective-C class, which means some things behave a little differently. To create an object from a Swift class, you need to explicitly call alloc and init, which are omitted when you use Swift:

```
//MyAwesomeSwiftClass subclasses NSObject

MyAwesomeSwiftClass *swiftObj =
➥[[MyAwesomeSwiftClass alloc] init];
```

You also need to use the message-sending syntax of Objective-C to call the functions of the Swift class:

```
//func doSomething(#number: Int, andString: String) -> String

[object doSomethingWithNumber:1 andString:@"String"];
```

To mark your Swift code as being compatible with Objective-C, you need to either subclass NSObject or use the @objc attribute. When you subclass NSObject, the compiler automatically marks the Swift code as compatible and doesn't require any additional steps. For Swift code that doesn't subclass NSObject, you need to mark the parts of the code that need to be exposed to Objective-C as compatible by using the @objc attribute. Here's what it looks like to create a class in Swift and use it in Objective-C:

```
//Swift:
@objc class MySwiftClass {
    var name: String = ""

    init(name: String) {
        self.name = name
    }

    func swiftFunction(string: String) -> String {
        return name + " " + string
    }

    class func factoryUsingName(name: String) -> MySwiftClass {
        return MySwiftClass(name: name)
    }
}


//Objective-C:
//@interface MySwiftClass
//@property (nonatomic, copy) NSString *name;
//- (instancetype)initWithName:(NSString *)name
➥OBJC_DESIGNATED_INITIALIZER;
//- (NSString *)swiftFunction:(NSString *)string;
//+ (MySwiftClass *)factoryUsingName:(NSString *)name;
//@end

MySwiftClass *swiftClass = [MySwiftClass
➥factoryUsingName:@"ObjC"];
NSLog(@"%@ Swift", [swiftClass
➥swiftFunction:@"Called"]);
```

Notice in this example that you use a factory method to get an instance of the class in Objective-C. This is because the Swift class doesn't subclass NSObject, so you can't use the normal pattern of alloc and init, and by using a factory method, you can let the Swift code handle the memory management. When a Swift class subclasses an Objective-C class, you have access to the `alloc` method and don't need to rely on a factory method.

 CAUTION

All the functionality of Objective-C classes is available to Swift when it is imported, but there are many features of Swift that cannot be exposed to Objective-C, such as generics and tuples. If you want to expose Swift code to Objective-C, make sure you are only trying to expose code that can be imported by Objective-C.

Being able to use Swift and Objective-C side-by-side in a single project means that you can incorporate Swift into an existing project easily, and you can also use Objective-C code to augment new Swift projects. This ability to work alongside Objective-C and the existing Cocoa frameworks makes Swift a convenient and powerful language to include as part of your app development toolset. You can use Swift to add new features to an existing app, or you can create a brand-new app using Swift. This means you can use Swift in the way that fits your needs without having to worry about losing access to your existing Objective-C code and frameworks when you choose to develop in this new language.

Exercises

1. Write a `UIViewController` subclass in Swift that contains a `UILabel` that displays the current date.

2. Write a Swift class called `DateAndTimeHelper` that is initialized with an `NSDate` and contains methods that return string representations of the date, time, month, day of the week, and year of the supplied `NSDate`.

3. Extend your view controller from Exercise 1 by adding a `UIButton` that cycles the `UILabel` through the current date, time, month, day, and year, using the methods in the class from Exercise 2.

4. Display the Swift view controller from an Objective-C view controller.

5. Write an Objective-C view controller that has the same behavior as your Swift view controller. This view controller should use the Swift class from Exercise 2.

CHAPTER 8

Common Patterns

Topics in This Chapter

- 8.1 Nested Types
- 8.2 Singletons
- 8.3 Using Grand Central Dispatch
- 8.4 Sequences and Generators
- 8.5 Operators
- Exercises

This chapter covers how to use Swift for some common programming patterns and tasks you may be familiar with if you are currently using Objective-C. You can use most of these examples in your code with minimal changes.

These are the key points in this chapter:

- You can nest types inside each other to make cleaner code.

- You can use soft singletons to create shared objects in an app.

- Using Grand Central Dispatch (GCD) is an easy and very effective way to manage threading and concurrent tasks.

- You can use `SequenceType` and `GeneratorType` as enumerators to iterate through custom data structures and also to produce independent sequences unrelated to any specific data structure.

- You can overload operators to work with new data types.

- You can create custom operators to perform operations on new or existing data types.

8.1 Nested Types

Swift allows you to define classes, structs, and/or enumerations inside any of those types, inside a function, or even inside a closure. A type defined inside another data structure like this is a *nested type*. Nested types help you to write well-organized and easier-to-maintain code. For example, a type that requires another type in order to function correctly can have that second type nested in it.

An address book, for example, could have a class to store contacts data. A person's data is quite complex, and a piece of data that may appear to be a single entry may benefit from being broken up into smaller components, such as a phone number, which can be broken up into its country code, area code, and local segment. By using nested types, you can define complex data structures in a clear and concise way. Here's an example of defining nested types inside a class:

```
class ContactType {
    //Define nested types
    enum PrefixType {
        case Mr
        case Ms
        case Dr
        case NoPrefix
    }


    struct PhoneNumberType {
        var countryCode: String = ""
        var areaCode: String = ""
        var localCode: String = ""
    }


    //Define local properties
    var prefix: PrefixType = .NoPrefix
    var firstName: String = ""
    var lastName: String = ""
    var daytimePhone: PhoneNumberType = PhoneNumberType()
    var eveningPhone: PhoneNumberType = PhoneNumberType()
}
```

Now you can create an instance of the ContactType class and set the properties as required:

```
var myContact = ContactType()
myContact.prefix = .Ms
myContact.firstName = "Kara"
myContact.lastName = "Thrace"
myContact.daytimePhone = ContactType.PhoneNumberType(
➥countryCode: "1", areaCode: "555", localCode: "555-5555")
```

Notice how the nested `enum` and `struct` defined within `ContactType` make those properties easier to understand, while keeping all the required information within the enclosing class.

When you need to refer to a nested type by name, you prefix the name with its enclosing type names, as you can see above with the `daytimePhone` property. Recall that because of type inference, when setting a property that is an enumeration, such as the `prefix` property above, you can omit the type name and just include the specific value, such as `.Ms` in this case.

If required, you can create an instance of a nested type that exists independently of its enclosing types:

```
var missedCall = ContactType.PhoneNumberType(countryCode:
➥"1", areaCode: "555", localCode: "555-5555")
```

Here, `missedCall` represents a single phone number; it's not dependent on any specific contact. You can nest types many levels deep if it makes your code easier to read and maintain.

 NOTE

The access modifiers `private`, `internal`, and `public` that are covered in Chapter 3, "Objects and Classes," affect whether a nested type is available for you to use.

8.2 Singletons

A *singleton* is an instance of a class where only one instance can exist. There are two types of singletons:

- A *true*, or *strict*, singleton has code in place to absolutely prevent a second instance from being created.

- A *soft* singleton, it's technically possible to create a second instance, but by convention, you just create one shared instance, stored in a `static` variable.

The soft singleton is the most common type, and it's the type we're going to look at here.

In Swift, classes cannot have `static` variables (yet). Structures, on the other hand, can have `static` variables, and as you've just seen with nested types, you can nest a `struct` inside a `class`:

```
class MySoftSingleton {

    class var sharedInstance: MySoftSingleton {
        struct Statics {
            static var instance = MySoftSingleton()
        }

        return Statics.instance
    }
}
```

Here you declare a class-level computed property named `sharedInstance` that is the same type as the class. Inside that, you wrap the `static` variable you need in a `struct` that you've called `Statics`. The static variable named `instance` is initialized with an instance of the class. Swift uses `dispatch_once` behind the scenes when you're initializing any static (or global) variable to ensure that it's initialized only once. (You will learn more about `dispatch_once` in Section 8.3, "Using Grand Central Dispatch.") Now you can access this shared instance in code like this:

```
MySoftSingleton.sharedInstance
```

 NOTE

You could put the `struct Statics` outside the property's closure, just inside the `MySoftSingleton` class, and the code would still work correctly. When you put it inside the computed property's closure, it protects the static variable from being accessed or modified by other places in your code. This method offers even more protection than marking the `struct` as `private` because there's no way to reference the structure from outside its encompassing closure.

8.3 Using Grand Central Dispatch

Using *Grand Central Dispatch* (*GCD*) is a great way to easily work with concurrent code, such as moving time-consuming tasks to a background thread. GCD is an important tool for developing apps that take advantage of the multicore capabilities of modern platforms. Using GCD feels very natural in Swift because you can often take advantage of writing the code that will be dispatched to execute on a specific queue inside a trailing closure. The following sections look at some common GCD patterns in Swift.

8.3.1 `dispatch_once`

Sometimes you need to ensure that a piece of code is executed at most one time. You can accomplish this with GCD's `dispatch_once` function:

```
struct Statics {
    static var onceToken: dispatch_once_t = 0
}

dispatch_once(&Statics.onceToken) {
    println("Give me a ping, Vasili. One ping only, please.")
}
```

This is a little more convoluted than you're used to in Objective-C because of the need to enclose the `static` token inside a `struct`. The effect is the same, and the code inside the `dispatch_once`'s trailing closure will be executed only one time.

8.3.2 `dispatch_async`

A common task is to execute potentially slow code on a background thread and then return to the main thread upon completion to do something else, such as update the user interface (UI).

 NOTE

Just as in Objective-C, you should do all UI updates on the main thread because the underlying graphic APIs are not all thread safe.

The following code dispatches the main closure to the global background dispatch queue:

```
dispatch_async(dispatch_get_global_queue(
➥DISPATCH_QUEUE_PRIORITY_BACKGROUND, 0)) {
    println("In the background queue")
    //potentially slow code here

    dispatch_async(dispatch_get_main_queue()) {
        println("Back in the main queue")
    }
}
```

Once the main code in the closure (just a `println` in this case) completes, it will dispatch the second closure back to the main queue.

8.3.3 `dispatch_after`

A simple way to execute code after a delay is to use `dispatch_after`, as shown in this block of code:

```
let secondsFromNow = 5.0
dispatch_after(dispatch_time(DISPATCH_TIME_NOW,
➥Int64(secondsFromNow * Double(NSEC_PER_SEC))),
➥dispatch_get_main_queue()) {
    println("That was so 5 seconds ago...")
}
```

8.3.4 `dispatch_apply`

Some tasks that are repetitive can be set up to execute in parallel. A great example of this is when you need to download multiple images for an app. You don't want to block the main thread, so the downloads should happen in the background. It also doesn't matter in which order the downloads occur, so long as each one is processed. Here's an example of what this might look like:

```
let arrayOfURLs = getArrayOfURLsForDownload()
let myConcurrentQueue = dispatch_queue_create(
➥"com.example.dlqueue", DISPATCH_QUEUE_CONCURRENT)
dispatch_apply(UInt(arrayOfURLs.count), myConcurrentQueue)
➥{ (index: UInt) in
    downloadImage(arrayOfURLs[Int(index)]);
}
```

NOTE

It's important to ensure that everything in the closure here is thread safe when using a concurrent queue. Each iteration of this closure is guaranteed to execute, but the order is indeterminate, and, of course, some of the iterations will execute at the same time. The `println()` function we use a lot throughout this book is not thread safe. In most cases this won't be a problem, but if you were to put a `println()` call in the closure above, you'd end up with an unreadable mess of characters that would all print together.

8.4 Sequences and Generators

In Chapter 1, "Introducing Swift," you learned how to use `for-in` loops on arrays and dictionaries. It's possible to create a custom data structure in Swift that you can iterate through just as you would with a built-in data structure. To do this, you make your data structure conform to the `SequenceType` protocol by providing a method called `generate()` that returns a `GeneratorType` object. The `GeneratorType` object must provide an implementation of the method `next()`, which returns an optional of the type your collection contains.

Here's a modified version of the generic `Carousel` class we looked at in Chapter 5, "Generics":

```swift
class Carousel<T>: SequenceType {
    var items = [T]()
    var currentPosition = 0

    var count: Int {
        return items.count
    }

    var isEmpty: Bool {
        return items.isEmpty
    }

    convenience init(items: [T], initialPosition: Int = 0) {
        self.init()
        self.items = items
        currentPosition = initialPosition
    }
```

```
    func append(item: T) {
        items.append(item)
    }

    func next() -> T? {
        if self.isEmpty {
            return nil
        }

        let nextItem = self[currentPosition]
        currentPosition = (currentPosition + 1) % self.count

        return nextItem
    }

    subscript(position: Int) -> T? {
        if self.isEmpty {
            return nil
        }

        return items[position % self.count]
    }

    //MARK: SequenceType Protocol
    func generate() -> IndexingGenerator<Array<T>> {
        return items.generate()
    }
}
```

There are a few modifications here:

- You indicate that the class conforms to the SequenceType protocol.

- You've added a convenience init method that lets you seed new Carousel objects with an array as well as optionally set the initial position in the seed array.

- You've made the code conform to the SequenceType protocol by adding the generate() method.

In this updated `Carousel` class, you are passing the call to `generate()` through to the `items` array. This prevents you from having to implement your own `GeneratorType` object because you get to use the array's implementation. The effect of this, however, is that the sequence of items returned is always in the order in which they exist in the array, with no dependence on the carousel's current position. You can see the problem demonstrated in this example:

```
var seedItems = ["one", "two", "three"]
var exampleCarousel = Carousel<String>(items: seedItems)
exampleCarousel.next() //consumes the first item,
                       //and increments currentPosition by 1
for item in exampleCarousel {
    println("item: \(item)")
}
//outputs:
//item: one
//item: two
//item: three
```

In this above example, you would expect the `for-in` loop to start at the second item because you've called `next()` prior to the iteration. You can fix this by implementing your own `GeneratorType` that takes into account the current position of the carousel. The first thing you need to do is define a type that conforms to `GeneratorType`:

```
struct CarouselGenerator<T>: GeneratorType {
    var carousel: Carousel<T>
    var iterations: Int = 0
    var done: Bool = false

    init(carousel: Carousel<T>) {
        self.carousel = Carousel<T>(items: carousel.items,
➥initialPosition: carousel.currentPosition)
    }

    mutating func next() -> T? {
        if done {
            preconditionFailure("CarouselGenerator
➥already completed")
        }
        if iterations >= carousel.count {
```

```
        done = true
        return nil
    }
    ++iterations


    return carousel.next()
  }
}
```

Here you define a `CarouselGenerator` structure that conforms to `GeneratorType`. It provides an implementation of the `next()` method that returns an optional `T`, as required.

 NOTE

Notice that here you use a struct and not a class. This is because you want the option to copy a `GeneratorType` object and iterate with the original and the copy independently. Had you used a class, multiple copies would be references, and thus iterating with one would alter the current position on them all, resulting in undesired results.

There are three properties in this structure. The `carousel` property is a copy of the `carousel` you're iterating through. You create this copy in the `init()` method, seeding it with the `items` and `initialPosition` of the original carousel. You use the `iterations` property to track how many iterations you've done so far. The `done` property is a flag to indicate that you've finished iterating through the `carousel`. A `GeneratorType` object should only ever iterate through once, and after that, calling `next()` again has unspecified behavior. You manage this with the `done` property, and you check it with each call to `next()`. If `next()` is called after you've already completed the iteration, you pass an error message to `preconditionFailure()`, as recommended by Apple. After checking the `done` property, you check the number of iterations you've already processed; if you've done as many as you have items, then you flag this as being `done` and return `nil` to indicate that there are no more items. If you still have more items to process, you increment the `iterations` property and return the carousel's next item.

Next, you can replace the `generate()` method in the `Carousel` above with the one here:

```
//MARK: SequenceType Protocol
func generate() -> CarouselGenerator<T> {
    return CarouselGenerator<T>(carousel: self)
}
```

This is how you create the `GeneratorType` object, initialized with the carousel you're iterating through.

Now you run the same test you ran previously:

```
var seedItems = ["one", "two", "three"]
var exampleCarousel = Carousel<String>(items: seedItems)
exampleCarousel.next() //consumes the first item,
                       //and increments currentPosition by 1
for item in exampleCarousel {
    println("item: \(item)")
}
//outputs:
//item: two
//item: three
//item: one
```

The `Carousel` now respects that you called `next()` before you iterated through.

In Swift, a sequence and its generator can be more than just an enumerator. There is no reason they need to be part of a known collection for you to iterate through. You can have standalone sequences that produce the Fibonacci sequence, random numbers, primary keys, or even records from a data store.

8.5 Operators

There are many built-in operators in Swift, such as +, -, *, /, =, ==, and so on. Each operator falls into one of three categories:

- **prefix**: The operator precedes its single operand (for example, `!true`).

- **infix**: The operator is in between two operands (for example, `1 + 2`).

- **postfix**: The operator follows its single operand (for example, `1++`).

Operators are processed in a specific order: `prefix` first, then `infix`, and finally the `postfix` operators. Each `infix` operator also has a `precedence` number to indicate the order in which the `infix` operators are processed relative to each other (higher numbers are processed first), and it has an `associativity` of either `none`, `left`, or `right` to indicate the order in which the operands are grouped. An `infix` operator can be optionally marked as an `assignment` operator if it will change the value of one of its operands.

Here's an example of the built-in += operator:

```
infix operator += {
    associativity right
    precedence 90
    assignment
}
```

 NOTE

You can see all the definitions by looking in the Swift framework's generated header. In Xcode 6, you can Command-click on any Swift keyword to bring up the generated header. The operators are defined at the top.

Operators use a function behind the scenes to evaluate their results. The following is the function prototype for +=:

```
func +=(inout lhs: Int, rhs: Int)
```

Because of Swift's type safety, this function prototype handles += only for the Int type. There are similar functions for each type that += is compatible with. Operator functions are defined in the global scope, not as part of a type.

8.5.1 Operator Overloading

If you create a type that you would like an operator to work with, you can create your own function with the correct parameters and then use the operator as you like. This is known as *operator overloading*.

If you wanted to use the += operator with your Carousel class, for example, you could create a function to append the right-hand side to the Carousel on the left-hand side. Because Carousel is a generic class, you can use a generic function that matches, and therefore it will be available to any Carousel object you create.

In the following code, you create a generic function that takes a Carousel<T> as the left-hand side (lhs) operand and a plain T as the right-hand side (rhs) operand. The lhs parameter is marked as inout because += is an assignment operator, and you're going to modify the variable in that position by appending whatever you get on the right-hand side of the operator:

```
func +=<T>(inout lhs:Carousel<T>, rhs:T) {
    lhs.append(rhs)
}

var seedItems = ["one", "two", "three"]
```

```
var exampleCarousel = Carousel<String>(items: seedItems)
exampleCarousel += "four"
//exampleCarousel: one, two, three, four
```

 CAUTION

You need to be very careful when deciding to overload an operator because you want to create code that is easy to read and maintain—not just for your future self but also for anyone else on the project and anyone who joins the project later.

The general rule of thumb is to use an operator only for a purpose that is obviously clear to the reader. If there is any doubt or ambiguity about what the operator is doing, it would be better to use a named function.

8.5.2 Custom Operators

You can go even further than overloading operators and create entirely new *custom operators*. This can be useful when an operator will help express the intent of your code in a clear and concise way. A custom operator consists of one or more of the following characters: -, !, ., *, /, &, %, ^, +, <, =, >, |, ~, or any of the Unicode math, symbol, arrow, dingbat, or line/box drawing characters. You can also use Unicode combining characters after the first character.

In order to create a custom operator, you must define what characters make the operator and whether it's a `prefix`, `infix`, or `postfix` operator. If it's an `infix` operator, you need to define its `associativity` and `precedence` and possibly indicate that it's an `assignment` operator.

The way you do this looks just like the way the built-in operators are defined:

```
infix operator ^^^ {
    associativity left
    precedence 137
}
```

Here you've created an `infix` operator `^^^` that will be processed with a precedence of 137, with its left side processed first. Now you need to create a function to actually do something when this operator is used. You can use this operator as a way of selecting the maximum of its two operands:

```
func ^^^<T:Comparable>(lhs:T, rhs:T) -> T {
    return max(lhs, rhs)
}
```

Here you use a generic function so that you can use this operator on any operands that conform to the `Comparable` protocol. The function just returns the `max()` of the two operands on either side of the operator:

```
println("1 ^^^ 2 = \(1 ^^^ 2)")
//output: 1 ^^^ 2 = 2
```

In the case of a `prefix` or `postfix` operator, the function will have only one parameter. You must preface the function definition with the keyword `prefix` or `postfix` in order for the compiler to correctly determine how to apply the function.

 CAUTION

As with overloading operators, you need to be very careful when using a custom operator. A future reader of your code likely won't have a clue what your operator is doing. Named functions are less likely to be misunderstood, so you should use custom operators only when they enhance the expressiveness of the code or when you're using an operator that has a well-known effect.

Exercises

1. Implement a primitive actor/movie database with records for trivia and famous quotes. Create two versions, the first with all the types as standalone (no nesting) types and the second using nested types when they seem appropriate. How do the two versions compare? Which looks like it will be easier to read and maintain in the long term?

2. Create a soft singleton object that could act as a theme manager for your app. Implement methods that allow you to query colors, fonts, and other metrics, based on the device type and size.

3. Use GCD to download an image from the web in the background and, once the download is complete, display that image on screen. Extra credit for creating a soft singleton object that can act as a cache manager to prevent downloading images more often than required.

4. Create a `SequenceType` that produces the Fibonacci sequence. Create another that produces unique string GUIDs that could be used as record identifiers.

5. Create a custom `prefix` operator that will take an array containing `Comparable` elements as its operand and produce a sorted version of that array. Create another that sorts the array in reverse. What characters did you use for the operator? Is this more beneficial than a set of functions that could produce the same results?

Index

F

factory methods, 132

failable initializer, 77

fallthrough behavior, 34

final keyword, 54

finding return type with pattern matching, 123

Float data type, 3, 12-13

fold functions, 116

forced unwrapping, 80

forcing requirements on associated types, 101

for-in loops, 7-8

for loops, 7

frameworks

  Apple framework, 120

  Core Graphics framework, 130

  Objective-C

    AnyObject types, 123-124

    bridged types, 126

    importing, 120

    primitive data types, working with, 129

functional programming patterns, 114-117

  custom closures, 117

  fold functions, 116

functions, 29, 103-104

  calling in Objective-C, 121

  closures, 112

    argument names, 113

    syntax, 113

  thread-safe, 141

  trailing closures, 113-114

  combining, 115

  customSort() function, 111

  defining, 104

  deinit() function, 120

  dispatch_after() function, 140

  dispatch_apply() function, 140

  dispatch_async() function, 139-140

  dispatch_once() function, 139

  enhancing readability, 106

  fold, 116

  generic functions, 26-27, 92-93

    syntax, 92

    type parameters, 93

    where clause, 100

  init(), 47-74

  nested functions, 30-31

  NSJSONSerialization.JSONObjectWithData() function, 123

  operator overloading, 146-147

  optional chaining, 85

  parameters, 104-105

    default parameter values, 107-108

    external parameter names, 105-106

    inferring, 113

    inout keyword, 109

    local parameter names, 106

    modifying, 109

    variadic parameters, 108-109

  reduce() function, 115

P-Q